CASE STUDIES
IN CHILD
AND ADOLESCENT
COUNSELING

Case Studies in Child and Adolescent Counseling

THIRD EDITION

Larry B. Golden

*The University of Texas
at San Antonio*

Merrill
Prentice Hall

Upper Saddle River, New Jersey
Columbus, Ohio

Library of Congress Cataloging in Publication Data

Golden, Larry B.
    Case studies in child and adolescent counseling / Larry B. Golden.—3rd ed.
        p. cm.
    Includes bibliographical references and index.
    ISBN 0-13-086818-3
        1. Child psychotherapy—Case studies. 2. Children—Counseling of—Case studies.
    I. Title.
    RJ504.G64 2002
    618.92′8914—dc21   2001021415

Vice President and Publisher: Jeffery W. Johnston
Executive Editor: Kevin M. Davis
Assistant Editor: Christina M. Kalisch
Production Editor: Linda Hillis Bayma
Production Coordination: TechBooks
Design Coordinator: Diane C. Lorenzo
Cover Designer: Paul Isaacs
Cover art: SuperStock
Production Manager: Laura Messerly
Director of Marketing: Kevin Flanagan
Marketing Manager: Amy June
Marketing Coordinator: Barbara Koontz

This book was set in Garamond by TechBooks. It was printed and bound by R.R. Donnelley & Sons Company. The cover was printed by Phoenix Color Corp.

Prentice-Hall International (UK) Limited, *London*
Prentice-Hall of Australia Pty. Limited, *Sydney*
Prentice-Hall Canada, Inc., *Toronto*
Prentice-Hall Hispanoamericana, S.A., *Mexico*
Prentice-Hall of India Private Limited, *New Delhi*
Prentice-Hall of Japan, Inc., *Tokyo*
Prentice-Hall Singapore Pte. Ltd.
Editora Prentice-Hall do Brasil, Ltda., *Rio de Janeiro*

10 9 8 7 6 5 4 3 2
ISBN: 0-13-086818-3

To Sarah and Martin Balleza, super parents!

Foreword

It was 1972, my first year as an elementary-school counselor. During the second week of school I enthusiastically visited each classroom, introducing myself to the children and engaging them in discussion about the role of the school counselor. My last visit was to a fourth-grade class. As I concluded my commentary with "and as your counselor, I am here to help you with your problems," a hand shot up in the front row. Before I could call on him, Jason blurted out, "My mom has been married two times and my dad has been married once and now my mom is getting divorced again and I don't know where I'm going to live. Is this the kind of problem you help with?" I took a deep breath. This was the early 1970s. Most of the problems that students had been describing were typical developmental problems that I knew how to handle. What Jason was describing was more serious and more than I had bargained for. I invited him to see me in my office, which was the beginning of our counseling relationship.

In reflecting on this experience, I realize how little I knew then, and how few resources there were for children in our school. We counseled children as if they were little adults, without taking into account that adult counseling models might not work. Over the past 25 years the field has evolved, and most practitioners who work with children and adolescents have specialized training and a wider range of resources.

Given the major problems children and adolescents face now as compared with 25 years ago, I shudder to think what it would be like if our field hadn't gotten "up to speed." Now a problem like Jason's seems minor as compared with those of some youngsters from my private practice: a 17-year-old who is winning the battle with an eating disorder she has been struggling with for five years; an 8-year-old with a conduct disorder who is in trouble with the law for destruction of property; and a 12-year-old who recently attempted suicide.

Without a doubt, growing up is more difficult than it used to be. In addition to the normal developmental problems, many children must cope with sexual abuse, divorce, poverty, alcoholism, abandonment, and violence. The number of young people who resort to self-destructive behaviors to numb the pain or to escape from their chaos is alarming.

Youngsters who do grow up in healthy families still struggle even under these positive circumstances. I am reminded of Matthew, a 15-year-old client. He is in psychological pain and he can't figure out why he is so depressed. The intensity of his feelings is frightening. He wonders if he is crazy when he is overwhelmed with negative thoughts. Matthew epitomizes the egocentric nature of adolescents, who believe that no one experiences emotions and situations as they do. It disturbs me to hear Matthew discuss suicide as a viable option. When I was a teen, suicide was something that I read about in novels.

The children I meet in these case studies remind me of my own clients. I've had to assess suicide potential as J. Jeffries McWhirter does in his case with 12-year-old Mark. In fact, McWhirter's comments about Mark's tendency to blame himself for everything reminds me of my client, Matthew, who also accepts too much blame. As I read Larry Golden's description of Joshua, the boy who trashed his final exam, I recalled the challenges of counseling a gifted teen and her perceived need to compete with her older sister.

Sometimes I wish we could return to the good old days when life wasn't so stressful and clients presented "Beaver Cleaver" problems. Of course, it's possible that I'm romanticizing the past. Nevertheless, we have to deal with today's reality. It is for this very reason that *Case Studies in Child and Adolescent Counseling* is a valuable resource for professionals. These cases were not created in order to neatly illustrate particular theories. Instead, they illustrate the complexity of the work we do with real kids. It's precisely this issue that makes this book so useful, and it impresses me that the contributing authors were not required to select a single theory or strategy and apply it exclusively.

As I read these cases, I was caught up in the step-by-step nature of problem conceptualization and the two-steps-forward-one-step-back therapeutic process. I found myself wondering if I would have arrived at the same conclusions and used the same approach. It was gratifying to overhear therapists in dialog with themselves, questioning and reflecting on what they might have done differently. Terry Kottman, for example, realized that she might have helped her client more if she had done couples counseling in conjunction with play therapy. Barbara Herlihy worried about whether her diagnosis led her to expect less of her client. In reality, we all have doubts about what we do. As Larry Golden observes, our field perpetuates the myth that there must be a magic cure. Those of us who do this work routinely know this is seldom the case.

Recently, I consulted with a colleague about an unresponsive 16-year-old. Just when I think Lindsay is about to turn her life around, she "self-destructs." It is as if she doesn't see herself as worthy of a good life and must, therefore, submit to her addictions. It is very painful to witness. I wish I had a magic wand, but there is none. On the other hand, perhaps the most intriguing thing about counseling is that there is no wand.

Marijane Fall notes that what energizes her about counseling is that her work and growth as a therapist are always in process. The creative techniques she uses are effective because she puts herself into the relationship; her presence facilitates the process. I remember as a first-year counselor being obsessed with wanting to learn techniques that would "fix" the client, but after years of practice I believe that who I am in therapy is as important as what I do. As I give myself permission to be myself, it is easier for me to connect with my clients and be, at times, a "salesperson" for how the counseling process can make a difference in their lives.

I predict that this is not a book that you will read just once and put on a shelf. You will refer to it frequently not only for assistance with a specific case, but also for inspiration.

Ann Vernon
University of Northern Iowa, Cedar Falls

Ann Vernon, Ph.D., is professor and coordinator of the counseling program at the University of Northern Iowa, Cedar Falls. She has a part-time private practice with children and families. Ann is the editor of a major textbook, Counseling Children and Adolescents, *and is author of* What Growing Up Is All About: A Parent's Guide to Child and Adolescent Development. *She is the author of the emotional education curriculums,* Thinking, Feeling, Behaving *and* The Passport Program: A Journey Through Social, Emotional, Cognitive and Self-Development. *Ann is director of the Midwest Center for Rational Emotive Behavior Therapy (REBT) and conducts workshops on counseling applications of REBT and child and adolescent development.*

Preface

I have to assume that my little casebook meets a need in the field because it's in its third edition. With each new edition, I've added and deleted cases in order to be responsive to changes in the counselors' working environment. In the second edition, I replaced five long-term therapy cases with ones that illustrated brief counseling strategies. Prevailing economic conditions favored short-term interventions, as they still do. In this third edition, I've replaced three private practice cases with ones set in schools. The new cases deal with *major* problem areas, such as sexual abuse, addictions, dual diagnoses, seriously dysfunctional families, and foster care. School counselors tell me that these are the kinds of cases that they are seeing. The sum is a balanced set of case studies that reflect today's practice in school, agency, and private practice settings.

I think it's significant that several contributors chose case studies from their early days of training and supervised practice. Some have included supervisors as co-authors. This should encourage those of us who train counselors. Those debriefing sessions with a supportive mentor, confronting personal issues, and even the tedious requirement to transcribe dialog have a powerful cumulative effect on the emerging therapist.

This is a hard book to organize because each case is idiosyncratic. It would be nice if I could pigeonhole each case as illustrative of a single counseling method, but real-life cases just don't work that way, so I've simply put them in order of client age.

There's a summary chart (following the table of contents) that allows an at-a-glance comparison of the 16 cases. For example, the reader will see that Suzanne M. Hobson, an elementary-school counselor, employs child-centered therapy to treat a 4-year-old boy suffering from post-traumatic stress disorder resulting from physical and sexual abuse.

Each case is organized as follows:

<u>Introduction.</u> The initial paragraphs lay out the presenting problem and background information about the client. The reader should know that in every case the identities of clients have been disguised. (This section is not titled.)

<u>Conceptualization.</u> Here the author discusses therapeutic goals and strategies. The author may justify the use of a specific theoretical orientation, such as Adlerian, systems, cognitive, behavioral. A rationale for diagnosis is also discussed.

Process. Actual client contacts are described. What happened in the sessions? How did the therapist's relationship with the client change over time?

Outcome. The author describes the results, for better or worse. I did not ask authors to present their most successful cases. I was after the cases that touched them.

Discussion. With the benefit of hindsight, the author explains what he or she might have done differently. In addition, the author describes personal and professional growth that resulted from this encounter with a troubled youngster.

Authors have provided their e-mail addresses (see "Biographical Statements") and have assured me that they would love to hear from readers. Take them up on it and get in touch.

I anticipate that readers will develop strong feelings about these cases. At the risk of waxing eloquent, I think this book beats with the pulse of living psychotherapy.

Acknowledgments

I gratefully acknowledge the help I received with proofreading from Becky T. Bean, a graduate assistant in our counseling program, and the expert assistance of production editor Linda Bayma, copyeditor Debbie Stone, and Executive Editor Kevin Davis of Merrill/Prentice Hall.

I would also like to thank the following reviewers for their comments and suggestions: Leslie Brody, Boston University; Amanda Franklin, Antioch University, Seattle; Richard James, University of Memphis; Susan James, Western Kentucky University; and Sondra L. Smith, Louisiana State University.

Larry B. Golden, Ph.D.
Associate Professor and Coordinator
Counseling and Guidance Program
The University of Texas at San Antonio

Discover the Companion Website Accompanying This Book

The Prentice Hall Companion Website: A Virtual Learning Environment

Technology is a constantly growing and changing aspect of our field that is creating a need for content and resources. To address this emerging need, Prentice Hall has developed an online learning environment for students and professors alike—Companion Websites—to support our textbooks.

In creating a Companion Website, our goal is to build on and enhance what the textbook already offers. For this reason, the content for each user-friendly website is organized by topic and provides the professor and student with a variety of meaningful resources. Common features of a Companion Website include:

For the Professor—

Every Companion Website integrates **Syllabus Manager**™, an online syllabus creation and management utility.

- **Syllabus Manager**™ provides you, the instructor, with an easy, step-by-step process to create and revise syllabi, with direct links into Companion Website and other online content without having to learn HTML.

- Students may logon to your syllabus during any study session. All they need to know is the web address for the Companion Website and the password you've assigned to your syllabus.

- After you have created a syllabus using **Syllabus Manager**™, students may enter the syllabus for their course section from any point in the Companion Website.

- Clicking on a date, the student is shown the list of activities for the assignment. The activities for each assignment are linked directly to actual content, saving time for students.

- Adding assignments consists of clicking on the desired due date, then filling in the details of the assignment—name of the assignment, instructions, and whether or not it is a one-time or repeating assignment.

- In addition, links to other activities can be created easily. If the activity is online, a URL can be entered in the space provided, and it will be linked automatically in the final syllabus.

■ Your completed syllabus is hosted on our servers, allowing convenient updates from any computer on the Internet. Changes you make to your syllabus are immediately available to your students at their next logon.

■ For the Student—

- ■ **Counseling Topics**—17 core counseling topics representing the diversity and scope of today's counseling field
- ■ **Annotated Bibliography**—seminal foundational works and key current works
- ■ **Web Destinations**—significant and up-to-date practitioner and client sites
- ■ **Professional Development**—helpful information regarding professional organizations and codes of ethics
- ■ **Electronic Bluebook**—send homework or essays directly to your instructor's email with this paperless form
- ■ **Message Board**—serves as a virtual bulletin board to post—or respond to—questions or comments to/from a national audience
- ■ **Chat**—real-time chat with anyone who is using the text anywhere in the country—ideal for discussion and study groups, class projects, etc.

To take advantage of these and other resources, please visit the *Case Studies in Child and Adolescent Counseling*, Third Edition, Companion Website at

www.prenhall.com/golden

Contents

Summary of Cases*

Therapist	Discipline	Child	Diagnosis and Problem	Strategy	Page
Suzanne M. Hobson	Rural elementary-school counselor	Boy, 4	Post-Traumatic Stress Disorder Physical and sexual abuse	Child-centered play therapy	1
Terry Kottman	Counselor, university clinic	Boy, 4	Phobia	Adlerian play therapy	8
Bruce St. Thomas	Psychotherapist, private practice	Girl, 7	Post-Traumatic Stress Disorder Unresolved grief	Art therapy; play therapy	21
Jules Spotts Jane Brooks	Psychologist, private practice School psychologist	Boy, 7	Post-Traumatic Stress Disorder Unresolved grief	Family drawing; "feeling story" technique; structured board games	34
Laura A. Granato	Elementary-school counselor	Girl, 10	School misbehavior Cultural issues Ineffective parenting Learning Disability	Structural family therapy	43
Arthur J. Clark	School psychologist	Boy, 11	Oppositional Defiant Disorder Underachievement	Person-centered; cognitive-behavioral	48
Barbara Herlihy	Counselor, private practice	Girl, 11	Schizoid Personality Disorder Social withdrawal	Person-centered	60
Larry B. Golden	Psychologist, private practice	Boy, 12	Dysthymic Disorder Underachievement Sibling rivalry	Family therapy; narrative therapy	70
J. Jeffries McWhirter	Psychologist, private practice	Boy, 12	Dysthymic Disorder Suicidal ideation, depression	Suicide assessment interview	81
Barbara Peeks Dunn Ray L. Levy	Supervisor Psychologist, private practice	Girl, 12	Conversion Disorder Psychosomatic complaints	Strategic family therapy	90
Vimala Pillari	Social worker, agency	Boy, 12	Conduct Disorder Explosive violence	Advocacy; supportive milieu	100
Kirk Zinck John M. Littrell	High-school counselor Supervisor	Girl, 14	Gang vendetta Conduct Disorder	Solution-focused counseling; conflict resolution	108
Dorothy Breen	Psychologist, private practice	Girl, 15	Adjustment Disorder with Depressed Mood	Family counseling; reframing	118
Marijane Fall	Counselor, private practice	Boy, 15	Depression Substance-induced mood disorder	Adlerian therapy	127
Scottie Sue Landess Nola Christenberry	Rural K-12 school counselor Supervisor	Boy, 15	Abuse Anger Depression	Team collaboration; consultation	135
Patrick O'Malley	Family therapist, private practice	Boy, 17	Maladjustment to death of parent	Solution-focused; person-centered	142

*Cases are listed in order of primary client's age.

CHAPTER 1

The Flight of the Lego Plane

Suzanne M. Hobson

Suzanne Hobson is the only counselor in a rural elementary school with a student population of 1200. Four-year-old Andrew presents with catastrophic problems. Andrew was severely abused by his cocaine-addicted mother. Andrew's prekindergarten teacher reported that he sat under his desk in a fetal position and, if provoked, lashed out violently. His behavior was consistent with Post-Traumatic Stress Disorder. Given the claims on her time, Hobson was tempted to use behavior modification, but chose instead, child-centered play therapy in a quest for a deeper healing.

S chool counselors rarely have the opportunity to work within the 1:250 ratio recommended by the American School Counselor Association (Campbell & Dahir, 1997). Responsibilities for implementing a comprehensive guidance and counseling program, including responsive services, guidance curriculum, individual planning, and system support, can be overwhelming.

Such was the case when I served as an elementary-school counselor. Although the school district was quite rural (the town had no stoplight or even a four-way stop sign), my school serviced a vast geographical area. Many students were bussed to the district, requiring upwards of an hour-long ride to and from school. The result: I was the only elementary-school counselor for 1200 students. Time was a precious commodity, and helping children under these conditions was difficult.

I first met Andrew when he was a 4-year-old prekindergarten student. He had recently moved into our district to live with a distant relative, who was serving as a temporary foster parent for him. Andrew was, without a doubt, the tiniest 4-year-old I had ever met. Small in height and slight in stature, Andrew's features sunk into themselves. In fact, serving so many children, the way I learned to first recognize this child was by his unusually small size.

Andrew's teacher explained to me that his behavior was problematic in the classroom, on the playground, in the cafeteria, everywhere. She described him as fluctuating between two poles: sitting under his desk in a fetal position or lashing out violently. Andrew's foster parent reported that he tended to either fight with her children, or more commonly, to completely withdraw from family interactions. She told me that Andrew had nightmares.

Conceptualization

I was tempted to begin immediately with behavior modification. However, I took my time and started with an assessment. Meeting first with the teacher and soon after with Andrew's foster parent, I asked about their observations and their knowledge of his prior experiences. I learned that Andrew was removed from his biological mother's care by the Children's Protective Services (CPS) because of abuse and neglect. He had been living with his mother, a cocaine addict, in a crack house in Detroit's inner city. His mother had sexually and physically abused him and CPS suspected abuse by others in the crack house. Ironically, in previous years, I had personally reported Andrew's foster parent to the CPS for suspected neglect of her own children. Although I worried about his placement with her, it became clear to me that she offered Andrew a safer environment than his biological mother had offered.

My diagnostic impression was that Andrew was suffering from Post-Traumatic Stress Disorder (PTSD) directly related to his experiences of abuse and neglect (American Psychiatric Association, 1994). His behavior seemed consistent with the three hallmark symptoms of Post-Traumatic Stress Disorder:

1. Re-experiencing: Andrew's recurrent nightmares
2. Avoidance behavior: Andrew avoided talking about the trauma and withdrew from interpersonal interactions
3. Increased arousal: Andrew exhibited angry outbursts, hypervigilance, and exaggerated caution.

In addition to PTSD, I believed Andrew was somewhat disoriented by the move from the inner city to a rural community only a month ago.

My goals were to provide a safe and caring counseling environment in which Andrew could express thoughts and feelings related to the abuse, to assist with the emotional healing process, and, yes, to improve his classroom and home behavior. Although it might have been more appropriate to refer Andrew and his foster family for counseling outside of the school, the reality was that the nearest mental health services were 30 miles away and the foster parent didn't own a car.

I chose child-centered play therapy. I had some excellent training in my master's degree program on child-centered play therapy, but my choice of method was based not only on familiarity with this approach but also on my feelings of being overwhelmed by the enormity of his experiences and not knowing where to begin.

Process

I arranged to meet with Andrew for 30-minute individual counseling sessions once per week. We met weekly for approximately 20 weeks during his prekindergarten year.

I distinctly remember our first visit. As we walked through the building from his classroom to my counseling room, I was struck again by his physical smallness. He walked without saying a word, arms flat against his sides and head downward. He responded only minimally to my attempts to initiate conversation.

On the way to my office, I asked an easy question, "So, Andrew, how old are you?" He not only didn't look at me, he seemed unaware I had asked a question. "You're not sure you want to talk to me. That's OK." At least he peeked up at me, but he said nothing. "It'll take some time to check me out."

I wondered what it must feel like to be a 4-year-old in this sprawling building. I began narrating our journey, "OK, we're going through the cafeteria. This is where the older kids have their lunch. This is the office, where the principal and the nurse work. We're almost to my room. I'll bet you've never seen anything like it." I was getting some interest.

As we entered the counseling room, Andrew's eyes lit up, but for only a second. I explained that children came to see me when they weren't feeling happy and that they could play in my room. Andrew walked the perimeter of the room, carefully inspecting it; no windows, bright colored walls and pictures of children, a loveseat, two small tables with child-sized chairs, and a corner partitioned off with a grown-up desk, phone, and computer. Here's the best part; a 15-foot built-in bookshelf filled with toys and art materials, with colorful curtains covering the bookshelves. Andrew cautiously inspected the content of each shelf: books, legos, blocks, puppets, art supplies, board games, and dolls and dollhouse.

I wondered out loud what Andrew would decide to play with, "There are so many toys. I wonder what you'll decide to play with today." I resisted the urge to offer direction, reminding myself of the importance of creating a relationship in which his needs were primary, in which his interests and desires took precedence over mine.

He then looked at me for direction. I offered none. We sat. With only a few minutes remaining, Andrew tentatively chose to play with the blocks. I thought to myself, "A noncommittal choice of toys. This is going to be tough." Our walk back to his classroom was once again filled with silence. I told him I'd come back to see him the following week. He reentered his classroom without acknowledging me. I had a few minutes to observe, and he seemed uninvolved in his classroom.

When I returned the following week, I prepared myself mentally for Andrew's lack of responsiveness. I reminded myself that he had learned the hard way that people who seem friendly aren't always so benign and that a good way to protect himself is to be invisible. I went to his desk and said in my most enthusiastic voice,

"Hi, Andrew! It's time to come play in my room again." He looked up and walked obediently to the door. Our long walk to my room was once again filled with my narration of the journey, but I noticed that Andrew looked around more as we walked.

As we arrived at my room, Andrew stood just inside the door. I stood behind him as if to say that it would be Andrew who led the way.

Counselor: Here we are again! Lots of toys and you can choose what you want to play with here.

Andrew: (*After doing a thorough inspection and then bringing the blocks over to the table.*) Let's sit here.

He spoke! He uttered these three words in a voice as timid and slight as his stature.

Counselor: Yes! I'd like to sit here with you as you play with the blocks.

Andrew began building very carefully. He pondered the choice of each individual block. He seemed to consider the size, shape, and color of each block before making his selection. Then, delicately, Andrew would place the block. I said, "You chose a green block this time," or "You're putting that block on top," and I played with the blocks myself.

Week after week, Andrew played with blocks. He became comfortable with me and my room. He'd smile when I arrived at his classroom and run to the door. Approximately seven weeks into our work together, he even reached out for my hand and held it as we walked.

In spite of this progress, I was impatient. I was supposed to be *helping* Andrew heal from the wounds of abuse and neglect, and all he wanted to do was play with blocks! As the weeks passed, I caught myself wanting to pressure him to talk about "it," to get to the issue. I wanted to say things like "I know some people have hurt you very badly, but you're going to be OK." Intuitively, I reminded myself to trust the process. I reminded myself that play is a child's language and to listen to his play. I reminded myself that my words would likely sound hollow in the face of his past traumas.

Eventually, a theme emerged into my awareness. Each week, as Andrew played with those blocks, he'd diligently build towers. As the tower grew and grew, Andrew would say proudly, "Look how tall mine is!" and would smile as he compared his tower to the figure I was building beside him. Aha! These blocks didn't represent noncommittal play (as I'd read in my textbooks). They had become his self-object! Andrew, the tiniest of tiny children, was apparently communicating concern about his smallness.

Reminding myself not to "help" him with the adult language of words, I intervened instead with the language of play. For the next two weeks, I consciously built various sized structures beside Andrew. I'd comment, "Look how tall this one is! Someone can see a long way from the top of it!" or "Look at this one! It's short, but it's sturdy. It won't fall down when I wiggle the table. Watch!" I'd wiggle the table and we'd watch the tall arrangements topple and the shorter ones remain standing. And then we'd giggle.

The next week, without explanation, Andrew decided to no longer play with the blocks. He surveyed the bookshelf and selected my Lego collection. Given my very modest budget for supplies, this Lego "collection" was limited to two airplanes and a boat from McDonald's Happy Meals.

Counselor:	Oh! You're not going to play with the blocks now. You've decided on the Legos!
Andrew:	Yeah.

Andrew built airplanes with the Legos, and week after week we engaged again in parallel play, building and flying Lego airplanes.

Andrew:	I'm building an airplane. Watch!
Counselor:	You're putting on the wings now.
Andrew:	(*With a look of concentration and a deliberateness of action.*) Yes, the wings have to go on now.
Counselor:	And there they are.

Around and around the room Andrew and I would fly.

Andrew:	OK. Here's yours. We're going to fly now.
Counselor:	Up we go!
Andrew:	Careful! Be careful! You're going to follow me.
Counselor:	I need to go very carefully. I'll follow you and you'll help me stay safe. You're the head pilot.
Andrew:	(*with arms extended as wings*) Vrooom!
Counselor:	I'm right behind you! Vrooom!
Vrooomm!:	(*The same circular pattern around the play area became routine, and each session concluded in the same manner.*)
Counselor:	Andrew, we have about 5 minutes left today.
Andrew:	Vrooom!
Counselor:	Vrooom!
Andrew:	OK, it's time to land.

During these flying sessions, Andrew would first very cautiously land his airplane on a bookshelf designated as the airport. After landing, he served as the ground assistant, helping me to land my airplane, "BE CAREFUL! BE CAREFUL! DON'T CRASH! WATCH OUT! CAREFUL!" When I landed safely, he'd breathe an audible sigh of relief and then remind me, "Don't let anyone touch these when I'm gone!" When I'd see Andrew between sessions, he'd ask about the welfare of his plane.

Andrew:	Hi! How is my airplane? Is my airplane OK?
Counselor:	Your airplane is safe and sound in the airport. I'm taking good care of it.

Of course, I was happy with Andrew's willingness to approach and speak with me but I still couldn't clearly relate what he and I did in the playroom to issues of abuse. As a fairly new counselor, I worried about what his teacher would think if she knew that we simply played blocks or flew planes during our "counseling" sessions.

I found myself pressured by a ratio of 1:1200 students and felt a need to "do something" to help Andrew. I told myself to trust the process of play, that play therapy yields positive results just as quickly as more traditional talk therapy (Landreth, Homeyer, Glover, & Sweeney, 1996).

One week, as we were flying our now very familiar flight pattern, Andrew added a new element.

Andrew: Follow me.
Counselor: Here I come! I'm right behind you!
Andrew: OK, now we turn this way.
Counselor: Turning, turning, turning. I'm right behind you. What a
               beautiful day for an airplane ride! (*Suddenly, Andrew threw
               his airplane to the floor. Legos scattered everywhere.*) Your
               plane crashed! (*I feigned horror in my finest reflection ever!*)

He looked up and smiled a special smile I remember to this day.

Andrew: "Yeah. But I can fix it!"

And week after week, he crashed and fixed his plane.

Outcome

Andrew's teacher, the principal, and the foster parent all came visiting, "What in the world have you been doing in counseling?" They indicated that Andrew was a completely different child in school and at home. He was playing happily and interacting appropriately during class. He had stopped hiding and stopped hurting others. I expressed delight at his improvements but explained that I couldn't possibly reveal our counseling interactions because they were confidential. I smiled to myself, knowing that they probably wouldn't believe me even if I told them.

Andrew had discovered an essential truth for himself. He had been deeply wounded and he could heal himself! I believe that through this process of play therapy, Andrew found this resiliency. I was still concerned about his current foster placement and what the future held for this little boy, but my confidence in his ability to make it was cemented during these sessions.

Discussion

When we ended our sessions, I faced the task of explaining to myself how it was that playing with blocks and airplanes led to such dramatic changes. In fact, I was able to grasp the depth of symbolism involved in his play only much later. I believe Andrew's choice of building blocks in the early sessions addressed his fears of inadequacy. Was his personal foundation (his building blocks) sufficient to withstand life's rigors? As he developed confidence that strength isn't directly correlated with size or height, Andrew was able to journey out into the world and back into his past.

An airplane flight pattern represented this journey into past experience. Consistent with my initial diagnosis of Post-Traumatic Stress Disorder, Andrew's play clearly reflected avoidance and emotional numbing (in his interactions with others and in his choice of play activities), hypervigilance (most clearly as we landed our airplanes at the end of each session), and toward the end of our work together, some reexperiencing of the trauma (crashes). He was willing to crash (face the abuse and hurts from his past) only when he had developed confidence in his ability to heal. Not surprisingly, it was at this point that Andrew demonstrated willingness in his classroom and at home to continue his journey into the future.

Why did I choose to use child-centered play therapy with this child and use more directive interventions with others? I realize now that I hadn't really trusted in the power of play. As a result, I tended to revert to using more behavioral, symptom-focused interventions when I wanted to get immediate results. By focusing on a child's behavior, I felt more like I was "doing my job" to help a child. What Andrew helped me realize is that I was more often making those choices to help myself (to feel competent) and to help teachers (with immediate, symptomatic relief) than to help children.

Andrew also helped me more deeply appreciate the difference between attending to the symptomatic behavior and attending to the underlying (real) problems. He helped me truly discover the power of play and to see the results of it, even though I continue to struggle with my ability to understand it. Finally, Andrew helped me redefine my job as facilitating such play. Although it has been many years since I have worked with Andrew, I often find myself reflecting on this case whenever I need to reestablish my trust in the play therapy process.

References

American Psychiatric Association. (2000). *Diagnostic and statistical manual of mental disorders: DSM-IV-TR* (4th ed., text revision). Washington, DC: Author.

Campbell, C.A., & Dahir, C.A. (1997). *The National Standards for School Counseling Programs*. Alexandria, VA: American School Counselor Association.

Landreth, G.L., Homeyer, L., Glover, G., & Sweeney, D. (1996). *Play therapy interventions with children's problems*. Northvale, NJ: Jason Aronson.

Biographical Statement

Suzanne M. Hobson, EdD, is assistant professor in the Department of Leadership and Counseling at Eastern Michigan University. She is an Endorsed School Counselor, a Licensed Professional Counselor, and a Psychologist in Michigan. A former elementary-school counselor, Suzanne continues her work with children at the Counseling Center of Ann Arbor. You can reach Suzanne at suzanne.hobson@emich.edu.

CHAPTER 2

Billy, the Teddy Bear Boy

Terry Kottman

Four-year-old Billy expanded a negative incident associated with a teddy bear into a full-blown phobia of all stuffed animals, dogs, and cats, and even bubble gum (Specific Phobia: Animal Type, DSM-IV-TR). Billy's mother was accustomed to previewing birthday parties and school activities in order to prevent any chance sighting of the feared objects. Terry Kottman uses an Adlerian approach with Billy. She sees Billy for play therapy and regularly consults with his mother. From this perspective, she frames Billy's phobic behavior as a bid for power.

We meet Kottman as a young and enthusiastic therapist. With the benefit of hindsight and years of experience, Kottman sees how she was intimidated by adult family members who were unwilling to examine their responsibility in maintaining Billy's dysfunctional behavior.

I was a doctoral intern at a university-sponsored community outreach clinic when I first heard about Billy Bass. When his mother, Darlene, called the clinic, I happened to be on telephone duty. She had a list of questions she wanted to ask about the qualifications of the student counselors who worked at the clinic. When she discovered that I was the intern with the most extensive experience working with children, she began to ask me a series of questions about my background, beliefs, and knowledge of phobias. Darlene wanted to make sure that the counselor she hired to work with her 4-year-old son had the "proper experience" because she had "diagnosed the problem as a teddy bear phobia." When she found that I had not worked with any young children who were presenting phobic reactions, she told me that she wanted to search for a more experienced counselor because this was "going to be a very difficult case to cure." This was fine with me. By that time

I was thoroughly intimidated by Darlene's barrage of questions and her seemingly impossible-to-cure child.

Time passed. I worked with many interesting children and their families during my internship. I devoted much of my energy to developing a method of working with children that combined the techniques and concepts of individual psychology with the practice of Adlerian play therapy. Every once in a while, when I was on telephone duty, I would remember the "Teddy Bear Boy," but I did not give him a great deal of thought.

About six months after our initial conversation, Darlene called the clinic and asked to speak to me. She informed me that she had not yet found a counselor practicing in the area who could meet her "stringent criteria of experience with phobic children." She seemed almost panicked. She said that Billy's phobia had reached crisis proportions: "He has gotten worse and we can barely leave the house any longer." I asked her to be more specific, and the story of Billy, the Teddy Bear Boy, emerged.

Darlene reported that until recently Billy had been the "perfect child." She said, "He still never makes a mess. He always does what he is supposed to do. He is not like other children. He is very responsible, respectful, and mature. He just has this one quirk that started last year and we can't seem to get him to stop." Darlene traced the "quirk" to an incident that happened when Billy was 3 years old. He was playing with a small teddy bear when he fell down and cut his knee. He screamed and cried, and his mother had reacted promptly with comfort and a bandage. His mother, wanting to help the situation, scolded the teddy bear for tripping him. Thereafter, Billy cried every time he saw the teddy bear. Eventually, his mother threw it out, but he started reacting with screaming and crying to every teddy bear he encountered.

Though he originally was afraid just of teddy bears, the list of things that frightened Billy grew and grew. By the time his mother called the second time, Billy was fearful of all stuffed animals, dogs, cats, talking dolls, and assorted other objects. When he saw any of these objects, either in stores, at preschool, or at other children's homes, he started screaming, crying, and shaking and would not be consoled. The only way to stop his reaction was to remove the object or to take him far enough away from the object that he could no longer see it. As time passed, Billy's list of frightening things grew even more, and he had attacks of uncontrolled hysteria more and more frequently. The situation progressed to the point that the family's activities revolved around the need to avoid teddy bears, stuffed animals, dogs, cats, talking dolls, and all of the other things that Billy feared. Darlene had started previewing stores to make sure that they would avoid the aisles that displayed teddy bears or any of the other feared objects. She also previewed birthday parties, other children's houses, and various preschool activities to make sure that Billy would not encounter any of the objects that triggered his attacks. Darlene wanted me to begin working with him immediately.

Before I met with Billy, I asked his mother to come in for a couple of sessions by herself. During these two sessions with Darlene, I began to gather some background information. I also talked to her about the fact that I would need her help in order to help Billy and the family. Although she really wanted me to "just fix Billy," I told her that I would need to see her for parent consultation every week. I would divide the 50-minute session between a 30-minute play therapy session with Billy and a 20-minute parent consultation with his mother. She was reluctant to agree to this, but I explained that she knew much more about Billy than I did and that I would need the valuable information only she could supply. I also pointed out that she could have a much greater impact on him than I could since she lived with him 24 hours a day, 7 days a week, and I would be seeing him only once a week for less than an hour. When I told her that I might need to see her husband and her mother-in-law, she said she would talk to them about this, but that she could not make a commitment for either of them.

Billy was an only child. Darlene had been close to 40 years old when he was born, and she told me during our first conversation, "Billy's birth was a miracle. We thought we couldn't have a child, but there he was, a beautiful baby." She reported that she had quit her job as a "very successful" accountant when Billy was born. She had decided to stay home to "be a good mother," and she was devoting all of her considerable energy to Billy's upbringing. Both of her parents were dead. An only child, she reported that she had never had much contact with her extended family. When I asked her about her activities and contacts outside the family—old friends from her job and the like—she looked confused. She seemed to be surprised that I would ask such a question and replied, "I really don't have time to pursue other interests. Taking Billy to preschool and his lessons and cleaning the house take up all my time."

The Bass family lived next door to Billy's widowed paternal grandmother, Estelle, who had retired when Billy was born to "help out." Darlene stated that her mother-in-law came over to "check on things" several times a day and had "very strong views" on how children should be raised. It seemed to me that Billy's mother felt that Estelle was more of a hindrance than a help. However, even when pressed, she would never confirm this hypothesis. Darlene seemed to have ambivalent feelings toward Estelle. She reported that her mother-in-law was rather critical of the way she handled discipline and had repeatedly expressed the belief that if she would just "whip him every time he carried on like that" Billy would stop reacting to the feared objects. However, Estelle was also the most consistent contact Darlene had with another adult. Darlene seemed to value the chance to talk about Billy and his problems with someone, even if it was someone who disapproved of the way she was handling the situation.

Darlene reported that Billy's father, Steve, worked as a troubleshooter for an international banking consortium and traveled during the week on business, coming home only on the weekends. During these weekends, Steve spent much of his time writing reports for the bank on his week's activities and drilling Billy on readiness skills—the alphabet, counting, and color names. Darlene reported that they had already enrolled Billy in a kindergarten class in a very prestigious private school for the following year and wanted him to "be ready to succeed in school."

When I asked Darlene about her relationship with her husband, she said that it was "fine." However, when I probed for details about how they managed to maintain communication and a level of marital intimacy, with her husband being gone so frequently, she seemed to get anxious and changed the subject. She would tell me very little concrete about their relationship. Asked specific questions about activities they enjoyed together during the weekends, she said they "spent quality time with Billy." She could not think of a single activity that they had done as a couple without Billy since Billy was born, even though Estelle always wanted to baby-sit.

Conceptualization

According to Adlerian theory, there are four goals of misbehavior: attention, power, revenge, and inadequacy (Dreikurs & Soltz, 1964; Kottman, 1994, 1995). From an Adlerian perspective, the goal of Billy's behavior was power. He used his fears to assert some element of control over others and his environment. There are two types of power-oriented behaviors: active and passive. Although Billy's method of gaining power had started passively, with his desire to avoid one particular teddy bear, his behavior had quickly escalated to a more active mode. By having hysterics whenever he encountered one of the feared objects, he discovered that he could control the decisions and behaviors of others.

In my experience, children who believe that they must be in control either have little power in their interactions with others—especially parents and other family members—or have an overwhelming amount of power in their interactions with others (Kottman, 1994, 1995, 1999). Billy had very little control over many aspects of his own existence. Either his mother or his grandmother still chose all of his clothes, dressed him, coaxed him to eat, cut his food for him, told him when he had to go to the bathroom, brushed his teeth, and generally kept him from making any move toward independence or individuation. At the same time, through his fears and the accommodations that people made for them, Billy controlled the actions of his family, most of the activities in his preschool, and many of the interactions in his small circle of friends.

Steve never attended a counseling session. Darlene reported that he was not available because of the demands of his job. Whenever I asked Billy's mother to bring Estelle to a session, she agreed to ask her, but she always arrived at the session with an excuse for her mother-in-law's continued lack of involvement in the counseling process. Consequently, I worked exclusively with Billy and his mother. I had five primary goals with Billy and his family: (a) to help Billy learn to express his feelings appropriately, (b) to help Billy realize that he did not have to use his fears to control situations and other people, (c) to help Billy learn new ways of interacting with others based on something other than the need for power, (d) to help Billy's parents and his grandmother let go of some of their control of Billy and let him have some appropriate power in his own life, and (e) to help Billy's mother cultivate some other interests in life besides Billy and reestablish an identity other than "Billy's mother." I assumed that once Billy realized that he could have control of many of the usual things 4-year-olds can appropriately control, he would not feel the need to use his fears to assert power over other people and situations.

▥ Process

Before my first session with Billy, I met twice with his mother. The initial session was a time for me to hear her story, assess the background and family information, and to begin building a trusting relationship with her. She had done a remarkably successful job of intimidating me when I talked to her on the telephone. Therefore, I decided that I needed to see her several times without Billy to establish some therapeutic leverage, so that she would not be totally in control of the course of therapy. One of the main things I had to decide during these initial parent consultations was the direction I wanted to take with Billy. My first response to Darlene's diagnosis of a phobic reaction was to consider abandoning play therapy and trying systematic desensitization or some other behavioral technique that has proven successful with phobias. However, as I talked with her, I realized that I did not agree with her assessment of the problem. An Adlerian interpretation of Billy's behavior as a bid for power made much more sense to me and fit with my theoretical orientation. I decided that Adlerian play therapy combined with parent consultation was a viable intervention strategy for the problem presented by Billy and his family.

Adlerian play therapy combines the concepts and strategies of individual psychology with the techniques of play therapy (Kottman, 1993, 1994, 1995, 1997, 1999). It is a four-phase process that first involves building an egalitarian, therapeutic, accepting partnership with the child. After establishing this trusting relationship with the child, the play therapist begins to explore the child's life-style. In Adlerian terms, life-style is a person's general orientation to life—the basic convictions about self, others, and the world and the behaviors based on these views that a person uses to gain significance and a sense of belonging (Manaster & Corsini, 1982). After developing an understanding of the child's life-style, the play therapist uses various therapeutic strategies to help the child gain insight into that life-style. The final phase of counseling involves a process of reorientation and reeducation. The play therapist helps the child learn new and more appropriate ways of gaining significance and interacting with others. In Adlerian play therapy, the counselor works with the child, using play media as a means of communication, and with the parent(s), using parent consultation and education, individual counseling, marriage counseling techniques, and any other available method of changing the child's social system.

I am not sure what I expected, but I was surprised at Billy's appearance when I finally met him. Billy was a slight child with great big brown eyes, an imposing frown, and an exquisite vocabulary. He talked and moved like a wizened 80-year-old man. I introduced myself and greeted him by name. I knelt down so that I could be at his eye level and remarked on the cartoon characters on the T-shirt he was wearing. I did this in order to disarm him because I was afraid that he would add me to his hit list of feared objects.

He did not seem timid at all. He frowned even more deeply at my frivolity when I asked him about his T-shirt and began to interrogate me about whether his mother had told me that he was afraid of teddy bears, stuffed animals, talking dolls, bubble gum (this was a new one since I'd last talked to his mother), and numerous other objects. I answered that she had told me and suggested that it was time to go to the playroom. We began walking down the hall toward the playroom with Billy continuing his nonstop questions and comments: "So, she told you that I'm afraid of teddy bears. Good. It's important for people to know that. I generally don't go to new places until she makes sure they don't have anything I'm afraid of there. You don't have any teddy bears or stuffed animals in this playroom, do you? You can't chew gum when I'm here. Neither can that lady at the front desk. Is she your secretary? Does she know I'm afraid of teddy bears and stuffed animals? If you don't remember to keep all of the things I am afraid of away from me, I will scream and yell and you will all be very sorry that you didn't do what I said." I reflected his feelings by saying, "You want me to know that you're afraid of all those things." I also began making guesses about the underlying message in his statements and his purpose in telling me all of this by saying, "You really want to make sure that I do exactly what you tell me to do. It sounds like it's important to you to be the boss."

When we got to the playroom, Billy did not look around the room to make sure that none of the feared objects were there. He stood very close to me and reiterated the entire list of things he feared. He also listed all of the situations that he found intolerable and what happened when he encountered any of them and told how it was his mother's job to "make sure I don't even see any of those things." He did this without breaking eye contact or taking a breath. I had decided to take all of the toys on the original list out of the playroom, and none of the toys that were left in the playroom were on the expanded list of forbidden objects.

Billy continued this pattern for the first four or five sessions. He was extremely serious, never smiling or showing any kind of emotion. He had the most intense eye contact I have ever experienced—he always looked me straight in the eye. He talked nonstop about all the terribly frightening things in the world and how "everyone" must help him avoid them. He described these terrifying things and his reactions to them in a flat voice, with no facial expression or body language indicating any kind of emotion. Although I usually ask children why their parents have brought them to play therapy, there was no reason to ask Billy. He repeatedly told me that the play therapy was "supposed to make me stop being afraid of things, but I don't think you can."

I used these sessions to begin to build a relationship with Billy. Most of my responses to him consisted of reflection of his feelings, restatement of the content of his comments, and guesses about the purposes of his behavior, which was almost exclusively designed to control my behavior and the behavior of other people in his life. As Billy gradually began to play with some of the toys in the playroom, he repeatedly demonstrated his dependence on adults by asking me to do things for him, such as turning on the water or opening the doctor kit. I made it a practice never to do anything for Billy that he could do himself, making encouraging statements that I believed he could do these things for himself. When he attempted to do things independently, I encouraged his efforts, regardless of the outcome of his attempts.

Billy very seldom did anything even close to breaking the playroom rules. When he did, usually by pointing the dart gun at me, I stated the limit in a nonjudgmental way, reflected his purpose (which usually seemed to be testing my reactions to his behavior), and encouraged him to generate his own alternative behavior by saying, "I bet you can think of something else you can shoot that would not hurt anything." Occasionally, he would complain that he could not think of anything else that he could do, but when I chose not to argue with him or try to coax him, he always thought of something else to do that was acceptable to both of us.

At the end of most of my play sessions, I tell the child that it is time for us to clean up the room together. I let the child decide who is going to pick up the various toys. I say something like, "What do you want me to pick up? What are you going to pick up?" This reinforces the need for action and builds a cooperative venture. Because Billy was so controlled, by his family and by himself, I decided not to use this strategy with him. I wanted him to have the experience of being allowed to make a mess if he wanted to do so without having to worry about an adult's reaction. I wanted him to experience the fun and freedom of being a child without feeling overly responsible.

As time went on and Billy began to feel more comfortable with our relationship and the playroom, he gradually expanded his repertoire of behaviors. He still did not play with many of the imaginative toys, preferring to play games and role-play structured situations. During this stage I continued to work on building a trusting relationship, but I also began to explore Billy's life-style. In order to do this, I asked him some questions about his interactions with his parents and his grandmother, trying to understand Billy's perceptions of his family atmosphere, his family constellation, and his method of gaining significance in the family. I also observed his interactions with his mother and his play in our sessions. Billy seemed to recognize that the family had an atmosphere of high standards, in which it was assumed that every member of the family would be responsible and achievement-oriented. He said, "I have to do well in school or my parents will be very disappointed in me." This statement seemed to produce a great deal of anxiety in him, and he stood very close to me for the entire session after he related this to me. Whenever he was playing, Billy watched me very closely, as if to determine how I was reacting to his behavior. He often looked at me as if to say, "Do I measure up to *your* standards?" I interpreted this to him by making comments such as, "Seems like you're wondering if it was OK with me that you did that. It's important to you that people like what you do. In here, it's up to you to decide what to do."

Billy told me many times that he was "the only son and the only grandson. That is a very important job." He seemed to feel very pressured by this position in his family. His behavior during the first two phases of counseling seemed to be almost a parody of the typical ways many only children act (Pepper, 1979). He was definitely the center of attention with me. On days when I talked to other children in the waiting room, he got angry and frustrated and talked in a loud voice, demanding my exclusive attention. He never talked about other people during our sessions, even the members of his family, except in the context of their interactions with him. He seemed to believe that he did not need to extend any effort himself to have things turn out the way he wanted them. He just needed to let the adults in his life know his wishes and he would get what he wanted. Whenever those wishes were not granted, he got angry and refused to cooperate. Our relationship was different from all of his other relationships. For the first time in his life, an adult was not controlling him or being controlled by him. He frequently seemed confused by my insistence that in this relationship we would share both the attention and the power.

Based on my analysis of his family atmosphere, birth-order position, and the goals of his behavior, I began to formulate some hypotheses that summarized Billy's life-style: "I am not very powerful, but I need to be powerful to be significant and safe. Other people are frequently more powerful than I am, and they will try to control me. The world is a scary place in which you are either powerful or powerless. The best way to cope with the world is to make sure that I am in control of myself and of other people."

Because I had now developed an understanding of the purposes of Billy's behavior and his life-style, I moved to the insight phase of therapy. My aim during this phase of the play therapy was to share that understanding in such a way that Billy could gain insight into his life-style and begin to make some changes in his behavior. I began to disclose what I thought were the purposes of his behavior, using tentative hypotheses to share my inferences about his need for power. I made guesses such as, "You really like to tell me what to do," or "You always want to make sure you're in charge and that things happen the way you want them to happen." He usually affirmed these guesses, sometimes verbally and sometimes nonverbally through a recognition reflex, such as a nod or a smile. However, when he did not affirm them, I chose not to pursue these statements. By not insisting that he confirm my guesses, I was letting him absorb the information I was trying to communicate at his own pace and in his own way.

During this stage of the therapy, Billy seldom mentioned his fears. He was a rather harsh and authoritarian teacher, and I was a compliant child. I used what I call the "whisper technique" when we did role-playing. This strategy gives the child control of the direction of the role-play. I use a stage whisper voice, which is obviously different from my normal voice and from my playtime character voice, to ask the child to direct what I do and say. For example, Billy would say, "I'm the teacher and you're the student. You will write on the board." I would whisper, "What should I say?" or "What should I do?" and then comply with his instructions. During these interactions, I would interpret his purpose in the form of tentative hypotheses, by making guesses like, "I bet you feel safer when you're in charge, telling me what to do."

We also played lotto and bingo at his request. He made up the rules for the games that we played. If he started to lose, he would change the rules to ensure his victory. Although sometimes I agreed to his changes and other ways of controlling our interaction, at other times I would tell him that I was choosing not to do that particular activity his way and suggest that we negotiate what we were going to do. Occasionally, I began to suggest that he did not always have to be in control, that sometimes it might feel good to not have to be in charge. He usually ignored these comments, and I did not insist that he acknowledge them or agree with me. I simply wanted to plant the idea that he did not always have to be in control. I continued to encourage his own strengths and ability to make decisions.

I frequently use storytelling and metaphors with children to help them become aware of their life-styles and to show them that there are different ways of gaining significance than their usual method of interacting with others (Kottman 1999; Kottman & Stiles, 1990). I asked Billy to tell me a story, so I could use mutual storytelling to suggest some alternative behaviors. He flatly refused to do this and insisted that he did not know how to tell stories. In a later session, I tried to tell Billy a story about a lion who got very tired of making everyone in the jungle do what he wanted by roaring every time they did something he did not like. Billy told me that it was a dumb story. He said, "That lion should have just roared louder and everyone would have done what he wanted." After this interchange, I gave up on trying abstract, metaphoric approaches with Billy and stuck to concrete interpretations and statements.

I began to point out similarities between his behavior in the playroom and his behavior in other settings. I made guesses about the fact that he probably liked to be in charge of situations at home with his mother and his grandmother and at school with his teachers and classmates. I also used tentative hypotheses to suggest that he was using his fears to control other people. His interactions with me were gradually changing, such that he was not always having to demonstrate that he was more powerful than I was. I wanted to help him generalize this behavior to his relationships with others, so I started making statements about the fact that he did not always have to be in charge with other people and he could still be safe and significant.

During these first three phases of the play therapy, I was also working with Darlene. We were focusing on her need to control Billy's behaviors, on her relationship with her mother-in-law, on reestablishing her personal identity as someone other than simply Billy's mother, and on her parenting skills. I tried to help her explore the underlying factors involved in her need to control Billy, but she balked every time I asked about her family of origin or made a guess about her own personal past having anything to do with her present life or her parenting. She would not acknowledge that her personal issues were a significant factor in her relationship with her child, her husband, or her mother-in-law. Since I was having difficulty getting past this resistance, I decided to settle for her agreement that her continued tight control over Billy's behavior would have to stop if she wanted Billy to stop having hysterics every time he saw a teddy bear (Kottman, 2000; Kottman & Ashby, 1999).

Although Darlene also refused to discuss the dynamics of her relationship with her mother-in-law, she did acknowledge that she felt hurt by Estelle's continued criticism and interference. She decided that she needed to establish some firmer boundaries to protect herself from this pain and to give Billy some relief from the constant pressure of having "two women telling him what to do." Darlene reported that she had requested that her mother-in-law not come over to the house unannounced and not do things for Billy that he could do for himself. She even gave Estelle a list of things that Billy could do for himself, such as choosing his own clothes, brushing his teeth, and deciding what to wear.

I wanted to help Darlene cultivate some other interests outside of Billy and reestablish her identity as a person in her own right. This would reinforce her willingness to let go of some of her control of Billy and his behavior. However, she was less receptive to these changes than she had been to the changes in her relationship with her mother-in-law. She seemed reluctant to try to contact former colleagues and old friends, saying that "they were busy and probably wouldn't be interested in my life now." I made some tentative guesses about how she was using Billy's fears and the curtailment of her own activities and interactions to protect herself from being vulnerable in relationships. These met with total denial and hostility. She said that she "just didn't believe that good mothers have interests other than their children." She did agree to join a "Mother's Day Out" at their church, and she also volunteered to do some of the accounting for the church. Initially, this was as far as she would go in letting go of her solitary role as Billy's mother.

I introduced Darlene to several Adlerian parenting strategies to replace the alternately autocratic and submissive styles of discipline on which she had previously relied. I taught her how to determine whether a problem was hers or Billy's and how not to let Billy's problems become her responsibility. I explained the four goals of behavior, the feelings that are the basis of the goals, and how to recognize them. We discussed the ways Billy was using his fears to gain power and to feel significant and safe. I suggested that she begin to encourage Billy for his efforts rather than praise him for finished products. I pointed out that she could use the same strategy she had suggested to her mother-in-law and not do things for Billy that he could do for himself. I taught her how to present Billy with choices, rather than always trying to control his behavior. I suggested that she use logical and natural consequences rather than punishment and taught her how to set limits and negotiate consequences (Dreikurs & Soltz, 1964; Lew & Bettner, 1996).

As Billy's need for power became less frantic, we moved into the reorientation–reeducation phase of the play therapy. Whenever Billy wanted to take control of the interaction or tried to control my behavior, I suggested that we use problem-solving techniques, such as brainstorming or negotiating, to reach a compromise solution in which we could share power. I encouraged him for trying to do things that he previously had refused to try, such as painting and making clay figures. I also encouraged him for making decisions for himself without trying to coerce me into telling him what to do or how to do it. He was much more willing to try to do things that were physically challenging, such as shooting the dart gun or hitting the punching bag. I pointed out his attempts at these previously shunned activities and his improvement in physical dexterity and self-confidence.

Eventually, with Billy's permission, I asked his mother to join us in the play-room. I modeled different ways of interacting with Billy for his mother. I coached Billy's mother through several different interactions with him. I encouraged them to begin to play together, to take turns sharing the power, and to negotiate solutions that did not disenfranchise either of them.

Although I had repeatedly suggested that Darlene needed some time to work on her own issues, she steadfastly refused to consider the possibility that she might need some personal counseling. However, during the reorientation–reeducation portion of our parent consultation time, we discussed her relationship with her husband and her feeling that she was "not a particularly important part of his life." We talked about her lack of friends and her loneliness. We also discussed the importance of having family time devoted to fun and togetherness, rather than to achievement-oriented activities. I pointed out that there was a relationship between these personal and family issues and Billy's problem, but she was completely unwilling to acknowledge that there was a connection. Despite her continued denial, however, she slowly began to make changes in all of these areas.

Outcome

Gradually Darlene began to establish an identity outside her identity as Billy's mother. She started taking several classes at a local university and made some friends. As Darlene began to "get a life," she gradually stopped living Billy's life for him. She let Billy take care of himself more often and let him make more of his own decisions. She got better at redirecting Billy's attention, rather than giving in to his fears. She also started setting limits on how much time she was willing to spend with her mother-in-law and on how much input Estelle had into Billy's life.

Billy also made some changes. He gradually became more like a 4-year-old boy and less like an 80-year-old man. He started to occasionally laugh and act silly. Billy began to play with other toys in the playroom by himself, without always needing to have me play with him. He made several friends at preschool, and his mother reported that he seemed "much happier, but now he makes some messes at home and doesn't always do what he is supposed to do." I took this as a healthy sign and tried to reframe this childlike behavior for her so that she could see it as growth in a positive direction.

Nine months after I started working with Billy, he began to give up his fears, one by one. Each week he would announce that next week he did not think he would be afraid of one of the things on his list of terrors. He started with bubble gum, even insisting that I bring some gum into the playroom so that we could each chew a stick. The last fear to go was teddy bears. Billy had stopped throwing tantrums in order to make sure he did not ever have to be near a teddy bear, but he was still telling his mother and me that he was afraid of them. Then one week, Billy went to a birthday party where the host was twisting long skinny balloons into animals. Billy decided that teddy bears made of balloons "weren't really the same as regular teddy bears" and brought one home. That was the beginning of the end of his very last fear. After Billy let go of this final fear, his mother and I decided that he need not continue to come to play therapy. Although I wanted his mother to continue to work with me, she said that she "really didn't see the point. After all, Billy is cured now."

Discussion

When Billy's mother first called, I envisioned myself having to develop some kind of elaborate behavior modification plan for his alleged teddy bear phobia. This never happened. As a matter of fact, we spent a small fraction of the many hours Billy and I were together actually talking directly about the issue of Billy's fears. The method of dealing with the fears from the perspective of the purpose they served in Billy's life worked beautifully.

I think I could have taken this strategy even further had I considered the reason for the family's willingness to cater to Billy's fears: By focusing on Billy's problems, Darlene, Estelle, and Steve could all avoid examining their own personal issues and the problems in their relationships with one another. Although I tried to address these problems with Darlene, I could have been more effective and efficient if I had worked directly with the entire family. I could have enhanced the therapeutic process by doing concurrent family therapy with all three generations of the Bass family.

As time passed, I realized that there were some obvious problems in the marital relationship between Steve and Darlene. I did not pursue this issue very strongly, and retreated in response to Darlene's reluctance to talk about their relationship. I could have helped Billy and his family more effectively if I had conducted some type of couple counseling in conjunction with the play therapy. Darlene was adamantly resistant to exploring her own family of origin and to having any other member of the family participate in the counseling process. By letting her decide who was going to participate in the sessions and letting her control what we discussed, I gave up a significant portion of my therapeutic leverage. If I had been more comfortable with owning my power as the counselor and had decided for myself who to include and the direction of the counseling, I might have had an impact on Billy *and* his family. At this point in my development as a counselor, I was still very hesitant. This lack of faith in my own therapeutic instincts prevented me from being as effective with this family as I could have been. Since that time, I have discovered that trusting my intuition and relying on my power as a counselor can enhance the outcome of the therapy process.

References

Dreikurs, R., & Soltz, V. (1964). *Children: The challenge*. New York: Hawthorn/ Dutton.

Kottman, T. (1993). The king of rock and roll. In T. Kottman & C. Schaefer (Eds.), *Play therapy in action: A casebook for practitioners* (pp. 133–157). Northvale, NJ: Jason Aronson.

Kottman, T. (1994). Adlerian play therapy. In K. O'Connor & C. Schaefer (Eds.), *Handbook of play therapy* (vol. 2) (pp. 3–26). New York: Wiley.

Kottman, T. (1995). *Partners in play: An Adlerian approach to play therapy*. Alexandria, VA: American Counseling Association.

Kottman, T. (1997). Adlerian play therapy. In K. O'Connor & L. Braverman (Eds.), *Play therapy theory and practice: A comparative presentation* (pp. 310–340). New York: Wiley.

Kottman, T. (1999). Play therapy. In R. Watts & J. Carlson (Eds.). *Intervention strategies in counseling and psychotherapy* (pp. 161–180). Philadelphia: Accelerated Development.

Kottman, T. (2000). Adlerian case consultation with a teacher. In M. Dougherty (Ed.). *Psychological consultation and collaboration* (3rd ed.) (pp. 48–62). Pacific Grove, Brooks/Cole.

Kottman, T., & Ashby, J. (1999). Using Adlerian personality priorities to custom-design consultation with parents of play therepy clients. *International Journal of Play Therapy, 8*(2), 77–92.

Kottman, T., & Stiles, K. (1990). The mutual storytelling technique: An Adlerian application in child therapy. *Journal of Individual Psychology, 46,* 148–156.

Lew, A., & Bettner, B.L. (1996). *A parent's guide for understanding and motivating children.* Boston: Connexions.

Manaster, G., & Corsini, R. (1982). *Individual psychology: Theory and practice.* Itasca, IL: F. E. Peacock.

Pepper, F. (1979). The characteristics of the family constellation. *Individual Psychology, 16,* 11–16.

Biographical Statement

Terry Kottman, PhD, is founder of The Encouragement Zone, a training center for play therapists. Before her "retirement," she was associate professor of counselor education at the University of Northern Iowa and the University of North Texas. Terry is a Registered Play Therapist-Supervisor and maintains a small private practice. She developed Adlerian play therapy, an approach to counseling children that combines Individual Psychology and play therapy techniques. Terry is author of *Partners in Play: An Adlerian Approach to Play Therapy,* coauthor with Jim Muro of *Guidance and Counseling in the Elementary and Middle Schools,* coauthor with Jeff Ashby and Don DeGraaf of *Adventures in Guidance: How to Integrate Fun Into Your Guidance Program,* and coeditor with Charles Schaefer of *Play Therapy in Action: A Casebook for Practitioners.* You can reach Terry Kottman at tkottman@cfu.net.

CHAPTER 3

Too Afraid to Talk

Bruce St. Thomas

Post-Traumatic Stress Disorder (PTSD; DSM-IV-TR) is a diagnosis that is usually associated with Vietnam veterans or adult victims of crime or natural disaster. Bruce St. Thomas encounters Kathy, an intellectually gifted 7-year-old client with PTSD who was devastated after witnessing the death of her younger sister. Subsequent to Kim's death, the parents' marriage broke up and the mother was hospitalized for psychiatric problems.

Over a three-year period, St. Thomas uses art and play therapy to probe Kathy's complex of blocked feelings, predominantly her sense of loss and survivor's guilt. Kathy's rich imagination becomes a powerful healing force and she is able to let go of guilt over not dying herself.

Kathy Peters, age 7, was referred to my practice by her parents. On September 7, 1984, I consulted with Kathy's parents, Paul and Joan Peters. They described the death of their youngest daughter, Kim. Kim was killed at 18 months of age when a car swerved on a major street that Kim, Kathy, and their baby-sitter were crossing. Kim was in a baby carriage that the baby-sitter was pushing. Kathy saw the car hit the baby carriage, saw her sister at the hospital, and was frightened that "she wouldn't wake up."

Both parents had observed changes in Kathy's behavior. Kathy was described by Mr. and Mrs. Peters and the school as being bright and mature for her age. Following Kim's death, Kathy regressed by being disobedient and babyish in responding to her parents. She became more distant and refused to talk about her feelings. Affect was markedly constricted. Kathy was fearful of being alone, frightened by the sound of sirens, and extremely nervous about crossing streets.

Her parents were concerned that Kathy had cried only a few times at the hospital and at the funeral. She also refused to discuss the accident, and her sleep was sometimes disturbed. Chiefly, the parents were concerned about Kathy's grieving process. External sources of information, such as school and friends, reported that Kathy was fine. No changes in Kathy's behavior had been observed at school.

High achievement was prominent in firstborn Kathy's early development. Kathy's motor, language, cognitive, and social development were all advanced. She had demonstrated leadership abilities in her peer group and was cooperative at home. She exhibited a high level of autonomy.

By way of background, Kathy's father, Paul, had four younger siblings. As the firstborn son, Paul had assumed a lot of coparenting responsibility because his father was away on business much of the time. Kathy's mother, Joan, was a middle child with an older brother and younger sister. Two years prior to Joan's birth, her parents had lost a female child at birth who had also been named Joan. Although Paul felt that he was favored in his family by his mother, Joan had a significant relationship with her father.

Conceptualization

I am trained as a play therapist, and my work draws on three major theoretical sources. My early work in counseling was based on a developmental approach (Erik Erickson, Margaret Mahler). Later, I was deeply influenced by the humanistic teachings of Rollo May and Clark Moustakas; in fact, I received training from Moustakas. I am also influenced by the field of art therapy (Judith Rubin, Edith Kramer).

I bring these three resources—developmental, humanistic, and artistic—to my work with traumatized children. I believe that all of these resources are necessary if I am to help a child conquer fear and integrate traumatic events. Furthermore, I believe that human creativity is the primary language for achieving personal insight and healing.

As a child psychotherapist, I knew that Kathy was not yet ready to reveal her inner feelings and thoughts. Kim's death had affected every aspect of her home life and family relationships. Mrs. Peters was hospitalized repeatedly for depression, and Kathy had been moved from one extended family home to another. Kathy found safety in suppressing feelings and thereby doing what she could to avoid any more emotional turmoil.

A therapeutic contract was established whereby Kathy would meet with me weekly to discuss any thoughts or feelings concerning the loss of her sister. I emphasized that anything Kathy shared would be confidential. Kathy would be consulted, and she would have the final say about disclosing any information, if I thought disclosure was necessary for her well-being.

I decided on a *DSM-IV-TR* diagnosis for Kathy of Post-Traumatic Stress Disorder. All of the classic symptoms were present at the time of referral. Specifically, Kathy showed constricted affect, feelings of detachment from her parents, reactivity to certain environmental stimuli associated with the trauma, sleep disturbance, avoidance of activities that aroused recollection of the trauma, and some guilt about surviving.

Play therapy was chosen as the method of intervention. Intellectually Kathy was gifted and successful, but emotionally she was highly defensive. The use of nonverbal play materials would be a means for promoting communication about feelings that could not be easily verbalized.

Process

Kathy was an attractive girl with light brown hair and blue eyes. She was neatly dressed and smiled frequently. She had good verbal skills and seemed comfortable in adult company.

The playroom was equipped with a hand-puppet theater, string-puppet theater, games, playhouse, sand tray, dolls, marker board, art table (with markers, oil and chalk pastels, paints, clay, crayons, and so on), stuffed animals, kitchen utensils, and a cabinet filled with other play materials.

Three or four sessions were initially devoted to an art therapy interview. I gathered information based on the child's responses to art and play materials, especially the themes of her drawings.

Kathy made an immediate attachment to a large, brown teddy bear. She picked the bear up and held it close while approaching the drawing table. I explained that we would meet for several sessions to draw pictures and to talk about her pictures and herself and her family.

Kathy:	I like teddy bears.
Counselor:	You are welcome to hold the teddy bear as long as you like.

I asked Kathy to draw a picture of a whole person. She chose color markers that had various fragrances. After smelling them, she began to draw.

Kathy:	I don't draw very good. This one is purple and smells like a grape. This pink one smells like watermelon. This is not a very good skirt. (*Kathy colored a sky with the light blue marker and drew bluebirds in the sky.*) They don't look right. I drew the birds like a letter *M*. I've done it wrong. This bird almost bumped into the girl. There is a fish factory nearby. I'm going to draw one because these birds are flying around it. This is a small fish factory made out of bricks. This is the ocean, and she is walking home after she went to buy fish. This girl is 7 years old. It's no one I know. She is thinking that the birds might eat her fish, and she is worried that the fish might fall out of the bag.
Counselor:	Kathy, since your first drawing of a person was a girl, could you now draw a picture of a boy? (*She quickly starts drawing with the color markers.*)
Kathy:	He is going to be at his house. His house will be made out of bricks. He lives like in a jail. There is going to be a lot of smoke coming out of the chimney. Me and my mother and father have always wanted to live in a brick house. Pink

is my favorite color. Now this big sun smells just like lemons. Mama, why does the sun smell like lemons? He gets to smell the sun every day. His pet bird is the only one in the sky. This boy is 7 years old. He is my boyfriend, Chris. He is thinking that the sun might never smell again, hoping that it will. He is jumping rope and feeling happy. (*Kathy continues to draw more bluebirds in the sky.*) He just can't be alone and needs more birds because he needs friends so he won't feel sad.

Counselor: Do the bluebirds help him feel better?

Kathy: Yes, they follow him and make sure that he is safe.

During the second session, I asked Kathy to draw a picture of herself.

Kathy: I have to make my eyes brown, pink mouth, and a black nose. I wish there would be a white marker because it would smell like marshmallows. Pink is my favorite color. It's not yours because it's a girl's color. I'm going to color my dress yellow so I will look like the sun. I'm going to try to make two ponytails. My daddy does my hair sometimes.

Counselor: Could you draw a picture of yourself and your family with everyone doing something?

Kathy: My daddy is big. My mommy has blonde hair. My daddy has short brown hair and I have long brown hair. My hair color is more like daddy. I look like daddy.

Counselor: What do you miss about Kim not being with your family?

Kathy: I miss everything about Kim. It is hard to talk about Kim. We don't talk a lot about her. I feel sad about it whenever I think about it.

Counselor: It is hard for you to remember things about your sister.

Kathy: Yes, I don't like thinking about her. (*Kathy completes her family drawing. See Figure 3-1.*) We are all going out to eat. My mommy, my daddy, and me are all dressed up. Mommy gets the most upset about Kim. Dad is the strongest because he is still going to work. I'm talking baby talk.

During the third session, Kathy drew a picture of her mother and father's room. She placed herself in her room with a friend. Then she drew her baby sister in her room with what look like toys. Kathy also used the puppets. She played with a squeaking duck who cried out to its mother for her to feed him and take care of him.

Kathy then returned to the drawing table, where she drew a picture of a house and some bluebirds in the sky.

Kathy: Once upon a time there was a little girl who lived in a little house. Four little bluebirds came to visit every day. (*I encouraged Kathy to talk about the little girl in the house, and she went on to dramatize the following scene.*) The little

Figure 3-1.   Kathy's family picture showed her mother and herself as equals. Kathy's deceased sister was not included.

girl was alone in the house and she kept crying for her mother. The bluebirds kept her happy with their visits to her windowsill. Inside the house the girl screamed that if the mother does not take care of me then I won't take care of her.

In summary, these early interviews with Kathy revealed several specific themes. First, Kathy was feeling the absence of her mother. At this point, in fact, her mother was in and out of a psychiatric care facility. Second, Kathy did not want to discuss her feelings about Kim's death. Yet she did make reference to the difficulty of thinking about it. Third, Kathy was perfectionistic about how she draws. Throughout her drawing activity, she often made critical statements about how she should draw or color better. Such statements indicated the standards she demands of herself. Finally, the bluebirds, as friends to both the boy and the girl, were symbolic of Kathy's need to not feel alone. Her many references to the sun, birds, and colors (pink and yellow) were symbolic of her yearning to express her feelings and conflicts. Kathy felt close to her father and yet interpreted his strength as being his ability to continue working. In family portraits Kathy portrayed herself as one of the adults in the family. Her need to not cause more emotional conflict was apparent.

I was surprised that Kathy immediately started drawing images that related to her feelings about Kim's death. In retrospect I can see that because we had outlined the nature of our relationship prior to the interview Kathy was ready to disclose. Her interest in the art materials, along with her ability to create story forms, allowed her to express feelings throughout the therapy process.

The following several sessions involved progressive play therapy interactions that moved back and forth between art, imagery, dramatic play, and verbal interaction.

Kathy's parents reported that she enjoyed her visits with me. At school, her teacher said that Kathy had become attached to her and wanted to hold her hand. Kathy had started talking about memories of Kim but was still unable to cry. She told her parents that she felt guilty about something but wouldn't say what. During the fifth session Kathy completed a drawing of two lakes surrounded by sandy beaches. Kathy filled the entire paper with designs drawn out to the border. She was careful to erase her errors and to color within the lines. Next, Kathy used fluorescent markers to create a drawing she called "Electric Basket." The marks were made quickly and yet were contained within the boundaries of the basket.

Three sessions occurred during which Kathy tried to contain and intellectualize her creative activities. In one session, she made a snowman out of clay. Her approach to this regressive material was restrained. She determined exactly what she would do with the material before she began to use the clay.

During a family therapy session, Kathy's mother made a strong effort to communicate with Kathy. Mrs. Peters talked about her own grief and emphasized that her depression was not Kathy's fault. Kathy's response was inhibited because she felt unsure about her mother's well-being and resentful of her emotional absence.

During the 12th session, Kathy drew another picture of the small house with a windowsill where the bluebirds meet the lonely girl.

Kathy:	There is a storm outside and the bluebirds collect on the windowsill. The girl opens the window and the birds fly inside. At first she is frightened. Later she realizes that the bluebirds are talking to her.
Counselor:	What are the bluebirds saying?
Kathy:	They tell the girl that the storm and the rain have frightened them. They are sad and scared. The bluebirds cry until the girl cries herself. The bluebirds tell the girl that they will protect her.
Counselor:	How do they protect the girl?
Kathy:	They make it safe for her by flying ahead.
Counselor:	So the bluebirds can see danger and protect the girl from going toward dangerous things?

Figure 3-2.   These bluebirds were Kathy's friends and protectors. They had magical powers and could foresee danger.

Kathy:	Yes, the bluebirds are with her even if she can't see them. They are magic and she can hear them all the time.
Counselor:	So the bluebirds are powerful friends.
Kathy:	Yes, and their magic powers now belong to the girl.
Counselor:	How does she know that she has the power?
Kathy:	The bluebirds give her a magic feather.

Sessions 13 through 16 were characterized by themes of magical powers of prediction and protection. (See *Figure 3-2*.)

In the 17th session Kathy played with the king, queen, prince, and princess puppets. The prince and princess were lost in the dark forest. The king and guard tried to find the lost siblings without success.

Kathy: The princess finally finds her way out of the forest. She is
          alone and keeps saying to herself that she is very, very

strong and knew her way all along. When she makes her
way back to the castle, the king is very, very happy.
Together, they summon the wizard who finds the lost prince.

Kathy continued the king and queen, prince and princess dramatizations
through the next three sessions.

Kathy: The king and queen had a daughter, Sally, and a son,
                  Benjamin. Benjamin and Sally were lost in the woods and
                  the king and queen tried to find them. When it was
                  impossible to find them they called for the bear guide and
                  the wizard to help out.

Kathy then playacted the wizard and the missing daughter. She made it possible
for the king to find his daughter.

Kathy: The only way that the children can be found is to go to the
                  wizard who has a magic wand and to put the children dolls
                  onto his wand. After the king goes to the wizard with the
                  children dolls, the wizard says that the children can now be
                  found because through magic. Maps suddenly appear in the
                  dolls telling where the children really are.

Meeting with the parents, I discovered that Kathy was becoming argumentative
at home. She angrily fought against time limits concerning dinner and going to bed.
Visits to Kim's grave site led to family discussions in which Kathy showed more
emotion.

Kathy drew a rainbow in session 21. She titled it "A Rainbow of Raining Hearts."
She drew colored hearts falling away from the rainbow design.

Kathy: I want to live at the end of that rainbow. If I lived there, I
                  wouldn't be scared all my life.

Kathy and I discussed her remaining fears about crossing streets, remembering
the accident, and seeing Kim at the hospital.

Sessions 22 through 24 saw a regression, with more baby talk and scribbling
with the markers. She declared that the last time that she was loved was when she
was a baby. Kathy invented a new name and a new character for herself, Katie
Allan. Katie talked baby talk. Kathy brought her doll and Kim's doll to the next
three sessions. In regressive play, she threw the dolls across the room. Then Katie
Allan talked with the wizard who placed magic blue powder on the babies so they
wouldn't get hurt.

The wizard knew where all the world's lost children were. By session 30, Kathy
was talking openly with her parents about the death and was sharing her tears and
grief.

In several of the family sessions, I had observed significant marital conflict. In
one of these sessions Kathy asked her parents what she would do if they died.

In another session Kathy played out a dramatic story involving a grandmother, Edith, and her granddaughter, both invented characters.

Kathy: Edith has a daughter who telephones for help because robbers are breaking into her house. When Edith goes to check out where the robbers are, no one is at home. The grandmother discovers that her granddaughter is hiding because she is afraid and does not have anyone to protect her. The grandmother asks the girl where her mother is. The granddaughter says that her mother is dead and that she has to kill herself because she doesn't love her mother anymore.

Kathy talked about ways of killing herself. Kathy and I then discussed her guilt and anger about the loss of her sister and her mother (Joan had been hospitalized for psychiatric problems).

Kathy's father moved out of the family home, and Kathy was again reunited with her mother who was now being treated on an outpatient basis. Kathy admitted to her mother that every single night she relived the accident.

At school, Kathy was chosen by her teachers as "best student."

Throughout session 32 Kathy's work revealed themes of displacement and survivor's guilt. She drew a picture of a person holding a kite. In the picture Oscar the Grouch is drawn on the kite and says, "Get out of here, scat, go away."

Counselor: Kathy, do you sometimes feel like you would like to go away?

Kathy: Yes, I feel like I should have been killed, not my sister.

Counselor: Somehow it would be easier to be dead than to have so many painful feelings about yourself, your sister, and your parents.

Kathy: Right! I would just like to fly away from here.

Kathy was upset about missing the previous session due to illness. She has become very attached to me and to our process. Kathy went to the window and talked about what it would be like to jump out. More discussion followed about her feelings of guilt and anger that Kim and not herself had been hit by the car.

In sessions 32 through 34 Kathy pretended to be a woman called Tutu. Tutu was concerned about her crying baby and spent a lot of time nurturing her. Kathy played Tutu initially but then switched roles to be the baby. She then asked me to play the role of Tutu.

In the 35th session Kathy drew a doodle of a person with a heart pierced by an arrow. The caption above the person's head said "I'm dying." Kathy talked about parallels between herself and her dead sister.

In session 40 Kathy talked about dealing with her parents' feelings.

Kathy: I would like to have a place where I could be away from their feelings. I saw a TV program where some penguins said, "Sorry for being alive."

Figure 3-3.   This flying tree symbolized magical communication between Kathy and Kim.

Counselor: Have you ever worried about being alive?
Kathy: I worry about dying every night. Sometimes when I say my
               prayers, I feel that maybe I won't live until morning. I
               pretend that I'm the wizard and I can ask the bluebirds for
               help. (*Kathy made a tunnel out of the cushions from my
               couch. During the next four sessions, she retreated into the
               magic tunnel.*) This is my magic house and when I go
               inside, you can't see through the walls. When I go through
               the tunnel, I am killed. I become a magic spirit.

Carrying in art materials, Kathy drew a secret picture in the tunnel. It was of
a magical flying tree with wings. (See *Figure 3-3.*) One time in the tunnel Kathy
regressed and pretended to be a baby. She also became a "magical princess" who
had powers to decide what will and what won't happen in her life. Kathy used the
flying tree in her magical rituals. The tunnel room became a safe place to regress,
as well as a place to be alone. I was told to wait for her safe return.

At times, Kathy involved me directly in her rituals. The flying tree became a talisman, a charm to bring good fortune when she sought answers to hard questions in her dramatizations. I could not help but feel the power of her self-directed use of rituals to repair her own psyche. My role, as facilitator, was to be sensitive to her leadership and to explore the symbols and metaphors that would arise.

During session 46 Kathy gave me a list of questions. She instructed me to ask the questions once she entered the magic tunnel. Some of the questions were about Kim. I asked the questions that she had written, and Kathy answered in a baby's voice as her dead sister.

Counselor:	Do you like living in heaven?
Kathy:	Yes, and there are angels here to protect me.
Counselor:	What do you eat?
Kathy:	We don't need food in heaven.
Counselor:	Do you still love me?
Kathy:	I will always love you. When you look up in the sky and see a bluebird you will know that I remember you.
Counselor:	What do you need?
Kathy:	I need you to know that I am happy. You should be happy, too.
Counselor:	Why did you leave?
Kathy:	Because it was time to go.
Counselor:	Can I see you again?
Kathy:	I will be in your dreams.

This and the preceding sessions involving magic rituals reflected the inner healing that was taking place in Kathy and in her relationships outside of therapy.

In subsequent sessions, Kathy dealt with adjustment to her parents' divorce and her father's remarriage, as well as Kim's death.

Outcome

Through art and play, Kathy replayed both the tragedy of her sister's death and the subsequent breakup of her family. Troubling questions were voiced in the drawings, characters, and animals that Kathy used as guides and enactors of the traumatic events. Kathy bonded with me and showed over and over again her need for nurture. She was not able to integrate concepts of safety and her own well-being until she had answered her own questions about the meaning of the events surrounding Kim's death. I was touched by her willingness, throughout the therapeutic process, to play with the feelings surrounding the trauma.

I continued to see Kathy and her parents throughout the next two years. The portion of the case that I have described speaks specifically to how Kathy resolved her feelings about Kim's death. Playing out an encounter with her sister provided Kathy with a means for diffusing her guilt over not dying herself.

Creating magical images such as the healing bluebirds, magical princess, and flying tree seemed to empower Kathy to speak the unspeakable truth about the traumatic event. I had to patiently follow and support her regressions and her mythical exploration. The patterns in these activities emerged only later.

Enough time has passed that I am willing to comment on long-range outcomes. Kathy made significant gains through the years. Her relationship with both parents improved, and she positively identified with her step-siblings. Her fears about losing her parents, step-siblings, and her own life diminished, and thoughts about suicide did not recur.

Discussion

Kathy's giftedness was both a strength and a weakness in her healing. Her cognitive ability was another defense against awareness of her feelings. Yet, within therapy, her inner explorations were inspired by a mind that wanted to resolve questions that could not be rationally answered.

From the beginning, this case posed problems in communication between professionals. Joan was in individual psychiatric treatment, Paul and Joan were in marital therapy, and Kathy was in individual treatment with me. Frequent communication between therapists did not occur. A team approach would have helped. Legal problems were another complicating and unpleasant factor. Kathy and Joan sought compensation for personal damages caused by the accident. I am not an expert in forensic psychology and must admit to feelings of dread when confronted with a subpoena for counseling records and the ordeal of appearing in court.

Kathy's story is a classic example of how the unconscious seeks expression through creative materials. Kathy's use of art, drama, and storytelling accelerated the healing process. Kathy was able to trust the therapeutic process when it became clear that I was genuinely interested in her stories and dramatizations. Through my work with Kathy, I have begun to better understand the concept of empathy as it relates to the child's play. I found it necessary to empathize not only with the child's verbalized feelings (animated world) but also with her nonverbal actions.

In retrospect, I was deeply touched by Kathy's ability to use a host of imagined players to create a very personal healing. I have learned from Kathy's deeper healing story and from other children's stories, that a community of people, characters, and animals are necessary to express the conflict and pain.

I believe that Kathy's stories have a universality that may be useful in other children's healing. Along with the individual's inner journey through the complicated grief reactions, there is also a need for community-based family support. Kathy and her parents would have benefited from a community-based grieving program. Today, centers for grief work are available as resources in many communities.

Transformation ultimately takes place when grieving children move from a sense of isolation and entrapment to a position of acceptance and well-being. Kathy and other children's abilities to speak of the unspeakable and to make sense of tragic life experiences has encouraged me to explore the deeper powers of imagination as a therapeutic tool for healing.

Reference

American Psychiatric Association. (2000). *Diagnostic and statistical manual of mental disorders: DSM-IV-TR* (4th ed., text revision). Washington, DC: Author.

Biographical Statement

Bruce St. Thomas, EdD, is a psychotherapist, consultant, and educator. He is a registered Art Therapist, Licensed Clinical Professional Counselor, and a Licensed Marriage and Family Therapist, (Maine). Bruce uses imagination, myth, metaphor, and art to promote awareness. He has completed large-scale visioning projects with The Children's Museum of Maine and The Center for Grieving Children and The Refugee Project in Portland, Maine. Bruce can be reached at bstthomas@cs.com.

CHAPTER 4

Oh No—Not Again!

Jules Spotts and Jane Brooks

A 7-year-old boy struggles against chaotic life circumstances with the help of two therapists, Jules Spotts and Jane Brooks. Early nurture by his maternal grandmother allowed Sean to endure the many losses he suffered in his young life. By the age of 11 he had experienced extreme poverty, a mother addicted to alcohol and illegal drugs, and the deaths of his grandmother and mother. He had never known his father, who was divorced from his mother during Sean's infancy. In the absence of any other family, he lived with a couple who were acquaintances of his mother and was finally adopted by a couple who subsequently separated. Small wonder the therapist who first worked with Sean (Jane Brooks) saw his reactions as consistent with Post-Traumatic Stress Disorder (DSM-IV-TR).

Brooks first met Sean when she was a school psychologist working under the supervision of Spotts. Sean's adoption meant relocating, which took him out of the school district in which Brooks worked. Fortunately, Spotts was able to assume the role of primary therapist following the move. Not surprisingly, the main issues of therapy were constancy, predictability, and continuity. The psychotherapeutic approach was augmented with the use of family drawings as a means of building continuity, "feeling stories" designed to help Sean label and express feelings, and structured board games that emphasized following rules and sequencing. Sean's adoptive mother proved to be an able partner in the therapeutic process, and the changes in Sean seem deep and enduring.

I (Jane Brooks) first saw Sean at recess. He was a spindly, wistful boy in a transitional first-grade class. He had been placed there because he was not believed to be developmentally ready for the second grade. He watched as the others played, peering at them with eyes that sought acceptance. Clearly, he was an outsider who did not know how to enter. He played with toys beside his classmates as though he were in nursery school. His only means of joining the group was jumping up and down. Any problem was met with an attempted smile that soon dissolved in tears if the stress continued. He was 7 years old and just beginning elementary school.

Gradually, in counseling I began to know Sean. By the spring of that first school year, it was clear that academic work was difficult for Sean, and he was referred to the child study team so that we could learn more about his learning style and psychosocial development. Since those initial school observations, I have been involved with Sean for some five years—first as a consultant, then as an evaluator, later as a therapist, and finally as a family friend. I have been the one constant person in his turbulent existence.

Sean was born in a small rural town several months after his parents divorced. Before their separation, for reasons unknown, the couple traveled extensively in this country. Family photos show Sean's mother as a stylishly dressed young woman. She had, in her youth, a life-style that included riding horses and a private secondary school education. Sean's father was a pilot who received a college degree during or immediately after a career in the army. There was a substantial age difference between the parents, with Sean's father being some 20 years older than his mother. Sean was small at birth, received appropriate postnatal medical attention, and developed normally. Health-care records indicate adequate care during infancy. What little evidence there was of Sean's early life seemed to suggest that the family had an upper-middle-class life-style.

Little is known of Sean's daily life before his fourth birthday, at which time he was living with his grandmother and mother in a residence for senior citizens in his mother's hometown. He attended nursery school for a scant few months. This unstable and rather unusual living arrangement resulted from his mother's alcoholism and Sean's need for daily nurture from a reliable caretaker. His grandmother was best able to fulfill this role. The family's well-furnished apartment had a living room, bathroom, and small kitchen. The grandmother slept on a hospital bed in the living room, while Sean and his mother shared a bed in the bedroom. Children were not permitted in the complex, but an exception had been made for Sean. His grandmother suffered from emphysema, was frequently hospitalized, and eventually died. Sean lost his home, and with it the security, consistency, and love that his grandmother had provided.

Immediately thereafter, Sean and his mother moved to a rooming house located between a funeral home and an automobile agency in a neighboring city. They shared bathroom and kitchen facilities with other families. The pair lived in a single room with one bed, a bureau, and a bookcase for toys. Linoleum covered the floor. Food was scarce. Sean describes eating cereal with water when there was no milk, foraging for cans and bottles on the beach and in the trash, and sitting outside playing in the dirt. Their next rooming house residence was near a small shopping mall where Sean was frequently seen playing unsupervised. In a minimally furnished room, Sean and his mother again shared a narrow bed, which he said had "springs that stuck into my back." He was often hungry and, in fact, appeared malnourished when he entered school.

By the time he was 7 years old Sean had experienced the extremes of wealth and poverty. He had observed a parent who could not defer gratification or plan for the future, but had also felt a grandparent's consistent love. He knew little of normal peer interactions or school behaviors. He wanted to learn but had difficulty concentrating. He was easily distracted, yet he wanted to comply and please. Though chronologically 7 years old, his interests and play resembled those of a 5-year-old. His intellectual level fell within the low average range, with weaknesses in sequencing, attending, personal knowledge, and immediate rote memory. Emerging strengths existed in abstract reasoning and understanding of social situations. At school, the child study team had added counseling with me and specialized academic services to his regular first-grade program for the coming school year.

Conceptualization

Initially, I chose the psychodynamic therapeutic process, believing it to be the best means of trying to compensate, to some degree, for Sean's rootlessness. I wanted to provide him with stability, security, and educational stimuli. Sessions during his first-grade year were concrete and reality-based and included teaching basic life skills such as memorizing personal information. Thus, my initial goals were to add more structure and stability to his life and to begin to build his academic self-confidence.

I continued to see Sean regularly in therapy during his second-grade year. Therapeutic goals for that year, which followed his mother's death, were (a) to address his need to mourn and to fully explore his feelings about his biological mother, including guilt about not liking her and his fantasies that he caused her death, and (b) to reinforce as strongly as possible his worthiness and ability to relate to others. In addition, he needed support to become a dynamic part of a new family. At the same time, it was vital for him to gain understanding and eventual control of his internal emotional turmoil.

Once Sean had parents to provide stability, my involvement and school became less important as constants. With continuing and dependable nurture at home, Sean was more able to focus his energy on learning. The psychodynamic orientation begun in the second year of our therapy would be extended. Key therapeutic issues at this time were Sean's fear of loss and his resulting reluctance to commit. My goals for him were that he become aware of his strengths and begin to trust.

Sean's move to a new school in his adoptive parents' community meant that he would no longer be able to work with me. However, this loss was somewhat mitigated by having a new family and the fact that my supervisor, Dr. Spotts, who was already very familiar with Sean, albeit indirectly, was able to serve as therapist in the new community. His initial therapeutic goal in working with Sean was to help him become aware of, label, and verbalize feelings. In addition, Dr. Spotts hoped that Sean would begin to understand sequence and cause and effect, and do some long-range planning.

Process

Therapy with Dr. Brooks

Sean and I began by telling stories to each other. Sean's chaotic life, his feelings of always being misunderstood, his dissatisfaction with life, his chronic exposure to alcoholism, and his intense need for security all became obvious.

In the spring Sean's mother became ill and died. Sean then lived with acquaintances of his mother, a couple involved with drugs, alcohol, and guns. Sean remained with them during the summer and for two months of the following school year. He then entered the home of his adoptive parents, where he remains. Therapeutic methods, goals, and strategies changed to accommodate his grief and new living arrangements. His stories now were about death, ghosts, and his own demise. His attendance at school and at his therapy sessions became erratic. I did not see Sean during the summer, but a psychological evaluation when school started again revealed poor impulse control, lack of trust in adults, anxiety, magical thinking, and denial.

Sean was assigned controlled, structured classes at school, which led to improvement in his academic performance. However, from the moment he left school until he returned Sean was in constant motion. He ate voraciously and constantly. His adoptive mother noted that he talked incessantly about trivialities. When he allowed himself to feel his grief, he was inundated with emotion. When his pain became too excruciating, he would vomit and then ask to be held tightly. It was only in the evenings that he could relax for awhile and was able to speak about traumatic events from his past. His intense, somatic reactions continued for several months, along with bouts of crying, sleepwalking, and nightmares. Sean's reactions were similar to the symptoms of Post-Traumatic Stress Disorder, not surprisingly, since his needs for stability and security had gone so long unmet. He felt exposed to chronic danger.

As early as December of Sean's first-grade school year, he began to tell stories at our sessions related to happenings at home. He revealed his feelings descriptively without labeling them and continued to intermingle dreams with reality, a confusion that escalated after his mother's death. His fantasies included being devoured by monsters and ghosts: "One kid came in there and he got eaten up by a monster." "The shark got his foot and then all the bones started to float up." He told of how objects came alive and killed him. Concurrently, there were glimpses of reasoning, conceptualizing, and reality testing: "Sometimes bad memories come and hurt us."

When school reopened in the fall after his mother's death, Sean seemed to feel the need to be punished for what he apparently believed was his role in his mother's death. In one of our sessions, he told a story of death and retaliation: "He stabbed the dinosaur and it died. And when he moved his claws he pulled the kid's eyes out and the kid died." Intellectually, he realized that substance abuse was the cause of her death. He said, "Crack is poison." But his feeling of guilt and fear of punishment were deep. Sean sometimes trusted adults and, at other times, was fearful, suspicious, and hypervigilant. His lesson from one story was "not to go near anybody that's going to hurt somebody."

Mutual storytelling was continued in therapy after Sean moved into his adoptive home. He continued to feel unacceptable, even evil, and was haunted by his dreams. He accepted nurture and love from his new parents but clung to them sometimes as though their love would come to an end. He continued to believe his own death was imminent, and he feared he would be taken away by the authorities. His stories and nightmares were about a bike being taken away, being eaten by a monster, getting killed by the evil in the bookcase, being burned by "red stuff" that oozed from the water fountain, and "running and running and then dying."

Although magical thinking and violence permeated Sean's work, over time his stories began to change. Most importantly, the main character assumed an active role. In one story, "when they fell asleep, the little boy broke the spell and woke everybody up.... Then everybody got bats and chased the witch onto a cliff and hit her and she ran off the cliff." In other stories a normal need for nurture and acceptance was intertwined with lingering concerns about accepting his new family: "And when he saw his grandmother with curly hair, he said it was really his aunt. You can't have a new grandmother. You can't really have a new grandmother."

Then, shortly before school ended, Sean told his first story about himself. "Once upon a time there was a little boy named Sean. On Friday he wanted to go to the grave, and he said good-bye to his mother. After Sean said good-bye, he was happy, and another day he had troubles and talked about them and then they stopped, and then Sean didn't have any more problems, and then he got more problems and more problems and that's the end." Questioned about these new problems, he said, "I had trouble on my homework.... I think I'm never gonna catch up with Mrs. Horowitz's class." During the last session for the year, Sean showed some contrition regarding being "fresh to Daddy."

Therapy with Dr. Spotts

When Sean returned to school in the fall, his adoption was not yet final. Sean began school satisfactorily, but by mid-October the nightmares reappeared. Therapy was reactivated, this time with Dr. Spotts, and Sean began to draw. He drew himself, he drew a train disappearing from view, he drew his feelings about his mom dying, and then he drew the courtroom where he would be legally adopted, as he envisioned it. The day of the adoption finally arrived, and he received the certificate showing his new name, which combined the old and the new. He now felt some degree of safety.

Following the adoption, Sean depicted his life in a series of continuous drawings in which he poignantly drew his feelings and struggled to label them. When we reviewed the paintings each week, he denied some feelings. Nevertheless, we persisted in this fashion for many months. Even with his denial, the process seemed to contribute to his emotional growth. The repeated practice of labeling feelings expressed in his drawings helped Sean stay in touch with his present feelings.

We examined specific emotions, particularly those that were regularly expressed in stories, pictures, and play. In many of Sean's stories, the main character killed someone—a person, a dragon, a witch—and then was killed. It was originally impossible for Sean to say what the character felt. Sean was action-oriented; he did not use feeling words or even acknowledge the emotions of his characters. "Feelings into words" became a kind of catchphrase in our sessions. Whether Sean was experiencing frustration at losing a board game or struggling with angry feelings toward a parent, he was encouraged to express his feelings in words. Gradually he began to talk about people's feelings, but he needed continual reminding and encouragement to do so. Any extended discussion of feelings was difficult, despite Sean's expanding ability.

Sean's parents were an important source of information about events in Sean's life, which helped us to address his academic struggles, peer problems, upsets at home, and other significant events in therapy. Three months after my work with Sean began, his parents said they had decided, after much serious marital trouble, to separate. Sean's home was suddenly threatened, and with it the security and continuity that Sean had begun to count on. The therapeutic focus was now expanded to include exploration of Sean's fears about the breakup and his newly learned ability to label his feelings. He was encouraged to examine his feelings about each of his parents as well as their decision to separate.

Board games had proven to be a reliable method for exploring feelings in therapy. The games were also significant vehicles in themselves because they could be used to teach and reinforce turn-taking, reciprocal participation, following directions, operating within an ordered framework, and exercising options with respect to making strategic moves. I hoped that these skills, once mastered, would generalize to Sean's classroom and everyday functioning.

Sean enjoyed the simple card game of War. This basic game allows for continuous reinforcement of order and sequence. At first Sean did not even know the sequential order of the picture cards. Further, War allows for extensive emotional exploration since the game has play-by-play excitement with little planning or skill required.

Sean also participated in the board game Sorry. We changed the rules so that each player was responsible for two colors rather than one. This game calls for planning, evaluation of several alternatives for each move, and a concentrated focus for an extended period of time. Early in therapy this game was not easy for Sean. However, he later came to enjoy the game, and often played for an entire session.

Given Sean's chaotic preadoption years, an additional therapeutic task was to provide him with a sense of order and predictability in his life and to help him find his own sense of order and control whenever possible. The above-mentioned games helped to foster a sense of order and predictability. The focus was on increasing and expanding the complexity of the game as well as elaborating and following the rules.

Throughout the game portion of each session—in fact, throughout the full session—Sean was unable to modulate his emotional expressions. As we threw a ball back and forth, Sean often whipped the ball far too quickly and hard (given the limited space in the office), laughed too loudly if I missed a throw, or complained too vehemently if he missed a throw of mine. Such overly intense expressions of emotion and episodes of crying also appeared in daily life, according to Sean's parents. Two basic techniques were used to help Sean with this. Careful pacing of activity allowed

Sean to experience a range of intensity and a smooth rhythmic flow of emotions in contrast to his usually spasmodic, irregular, and intense expression of impulses. I did this through very slow speech, thinking out loud when making game moves, and faking throws to model more appropriate ways of teasing or engaging the other player. In general, I modeled a variety of behaviors and kept changing the pace of our activity to illustrate the flexibility that Sean seemed to lack. Nonverbal cues, such as slowly lowering my hand, became a signal to Sean to slow down and regain a measure of control.

Outcome

Sean progressed emotionally and socially during the two years that he worked with Dr. Brooks. However, in spite of major gains, none of his critical emotional issues were settled when their therapeutic alliance ended. Sean needed more therapy to develop his reasoning, insight, and understanding further. His tensions and anxiety were decreasing, but his self-understanding and play were still well below age level. Too often, Sean could not differentiate, label, or verbalize his feelings. Through mutual storytelling, Sean began to see that a person could make changes in his life and that events did not occur simply because one thought about them. He began to see himself as a change agent in fantasy and in reality. He asked to switch from one classroom to another, and his request was granted. On another occasion he was verbally abusive to his mother and deeply hurt her. He was discovering that his actions had social and emotional repercussions, some positive and others not, and that he was able to control some events rather than being a passive recipient. This understanding resulted in improved peer relationships. Rather than being mystified or devastated by teasing from his peers, Sean began to make the connection between his behavior and the responses he received.

Sean's emotional and social growth continued with Dr. Spotts. Over nine months of psychodynamic therapy, Sean completed mourning and gained enough self-confidence and security to experience and express anger toward his mother and father. However, he still denied many feelings, relived his fears of abandonment, and met new stress by weeping. He almost always covered his emotions with smiles and later broke down. He could not modulate his feelings and was either too exuberant or too sad.

On the other hand, Sean was beginning to lead a normal little boy's life. Magical thinking was taking a back seat. He began to talk directly about his problems, and relationships took on a healthier, more appropriate tone. The therapists hypothesized that Sean had early on developed a basic trust in the world, largely through his relationship with his grandmother. The emotional inaccessibility of his mother and temporary caretakers elicited his defensive armor. With his adoption and the presence of a stable, nurturing home, as well as regular psychotherapy, Sean was able to build healthier ego defenses. Since the threat of loss had abated, Sean could use some of the energy that had been devoted to defending against loss to begin to examine his own behavior. He was less hypervigilant than in the past, able to relax a little, and showed more spontaneity. He was able to understand that his tendency to "overemote" was not working as he had hoped. Rather than attract others, this trait seemed to drive them away. Sean also began to understand that people were not simply "mean," as he had often thought, but rather that his own behavior could influence the treatment he got from others.

Sean was beginning to live an orderly life, to follow the routines of going to school, doing homework, eating, and preparing for bedtime, but an understanding of these cycles eluded him. In spite of working on the continuity and connections in his life (through stories, drawings, and games), the ordering and sequencing of information remained an enigma for Sean. At school he began to comprehend numbers but did not grasp progression and ordering. Whether he had a true learning disability or whether his chaotic life made this concept difficult remains uncertain.

Sean had begun to invest in emotional relationships with each adoptive parent and in the continuity of their home life. His parents' separation, the attendant uncertainty about their marriage, and the prospect of living in yet another home (the father's residence) were serious threats for Sean. Feelings of rejection and abandonment continued to plague him. All his loved ones or those he wanted to love had abandoned him, either by death or by choice. Loss loomed large for Sean. He was afraid, for example, that the state would remove him from his home, and he would scream out in his sleep, "Don't take me away!" In someone who has lived through so many changes and endured so many losses, a sense of security and self-worth can be rebuilt only gradually. Although Sean had made gains in both areas, controlling his emotions and improving his academic performance will continue to be important goals in the coming years.

Although the future unity of Sean's family remains in doubt, the therapeutic gains Sean has made seem deep and enduring. He appears to possess sufficient ego strength to continue his progress in the face of changes or discontinuities in relationships.

Discussion

We carefully formulated an overall, long-term treatment plan for Sean. The key themes in therapy were constancy, predictability, and continuity. Treating Sean at his school made sense initially, and when this was no longer possible because of his change in residence, it was fortunate that therapeutic responsibility could be shifted from Dr. Brooks to Dr. Spotts, who had been serving as her supervisor. Sean's fear of rejection and abandonment led Dr. Brooks to continue to see him, albeit irregularly, after her formal work with him had ended.

Sean's adoption into what had the possibility of being a stable, nurturing family was a rare blessing in his young life. With his parents' separation, changes in treatment became necessary. The use of family drawings as part of therapy was an attempt to help Sean create an orderly, sequential understanding of his life. Later in therapy, structured board games were used for this same purpose. These methods were only minimally effective in addressing this problem, so great was the impact of his early fragmented years.

Given Sean's denial of feelings and pervasive underlying anxiety, a primary goal of therapy was to help Sean identify and label feelings through the feeling stories. This technique, augmented with periodic input from his parents about events in their son's life, allowed Sean to begin to practice these skills. Sean's adoptive mother proved to be effective in actively listening to his feelings. Her acceptance enabled Sean to rely less on denial and suppression of feelings. Sean's growing feeling of safety with his mother allowed him to experience and express his feelings *about* her *to* her. This process has been slower with his father, but is under way. Despite the parental separation, Sean has not experienced significant regression, a positive statement about both Sean and his parents.

Reference

American Psychiatric Association. (2000). *Diagnostic and statistical manual of mental disorders: DSM-IV-TR* (4th ed., text revision). Washington, DC: Author.

Biographical Statements

Jane Brooks, EdD, is a licensed psychologist in New Jersey and a licensed professional counselor in Connecticut. She currently works as a school psychologist doing counseling, evaluations, and parent and teacher consultation. Jane presented a paper at the 1990 annual convention of the National Association of School Psychologists (NASP) and has written articles for the journal *Teaching Exceptional Children*. She was an adjunct teacher in school psychology at Fairfield University Graduate School of Education. You can reach Jane at jpb189@aol.com.

Jules Spotts, PhD, is a licensed clinical psychologist in private practice in New Canaan, Connecticut, and a consultant to the New Canaan Country School. He is coauthor of a book, *You Can Say No to Your Teenager* (Addison Wesley, 1991). You can reach Jules at bsil112@aol.com.

CHAPTER 5

Family Secrets

Laura A. Granato

Family secrets can block relationships, but can also be explosive. Granato believes that a secret trauma has disabled communication between husband and wife and, consequently, poses an obstacle to effective parenting for 10-year-old Esperanza. In her role as school counselor, Granato opts for brief marital and family therapy in an attempt to open up communication and promote effective parenting. Granato consistently employs the techniques of Salvador Minuchin's structural family therapy. She is sensitive to the effects of culture in counseling with this Hispanic family.

E speranza is a 10-year-old fifth-grade elementary school student in a large suburban school district near Washington, D.C. Esperanza attended the school where I served for two years as the only school counselor for 500 students. Esperanza was the oldest of three children from a bilingual (Spanish and English) family that had undergone considerable medical, financial, and marital problems since she was born. Teachers reported that the parents failed to follow through with suggestions made at conferences.

The classroom teacher referred Esperanza. She described Esperanza as uncooperative, refusing to complete schoolwork and to follow directions. On several occasions she ran away from the school building. She engaged in name-calling with peers. Sometimes she was bossy but usually isolated herself, perhaps to avoid rejection. Esperanza was caught stealing on numerous occasions. When confronted, she denied it. Esperanza exhibited severe mood changes.

Conceptualization

Esperanza's family was new to the school. No records were available to assess Esperanza's past school performance, except for paperwork indicating a learning disability. She was receiving services for auditory processing difficulties. I wondered how much of Esperanza's difficulties were due to her bilingual upbringing. The results of the dual language assessment indicated proficiency in English for her age and grade level. Since Esperanza's family had just moved to a new community and school I diagnosed her with adjustment disorder. Later, I came to see her symptoms as chronic.

I approached this case from a systems perspective. Prior to entering the schools, I had received training at The Philadelphia Child Guidance Clinic and learned to use structural family therapy concepts. Thinking about hierarchies and boundaries in families and institutions has really helped me in working in the schools.

The Lopez family needed assurance that confidentiality would be maintained and that other school personnel would not be privy to information disclosed in our sessions. This process of joining the family became my priority.

Process

The school is part of the child's system, so my initial interventions began there. I arranged for Esperanza to be assigned to a first-grade classroom to assist children with reading. In this way her "mothering" and "bossy" behaviors could be channeled positively. Following are accounts of my interventions with the family.

Session 1. I met with Gloria and Ernesto Lopez (Esperanza's mother and father). They sheepishly entered my office one morning after dropping the children off at school. We began with the intake and family history. We sat at a round table, and I could not help but notice how far apart the parents sat. I commented on their obvious anxiety. Gloria's response was, "in Puerto Rico we do not have counselors." I listened respectfully to their story of the children's behavior problems and their efforts at working with the school. We reviewed informed consent and they seemed offended by the exceptions to confidentiality, especially with regard to child abuse. She told me that in Puerto Rico, school personnel wouldn't even talk about limits to confidentiality. She just assumed that everything was confidential.

I asked about confidential matters they might be willing to trust me with. Gloria told me about her diagnosis of advanced uterine cancer. We agreed that in a session with the children, I would help her talk about this at a level she and Ernesto felt was appropriate.

Session 2. All family members were present: Gloria, Ernesto, Esperanza, Miguel (third-grader), and Arturo (first-grader). I asked what brought them in for counseling. "Because Esperanza is always in trouble," Miguel shouted. I asked if anyone else had anything to say about Esperanza and all shook their heads, indicating no. I informed the family that although Esperanza's difficulties in school were the reason they were in my office, I needed everyone's help.

Ernesto could read and write very little English and his preferred speaking language was Spanish. He talked with the children in Spanish. We agreed to have each family member speak the language with which they most felt comfortable. Ernesto opted for Spanish. Luckily, I am somewhat bilingual myself, and comprehend more Spanish than I can speak.

I asked each family member to complete a kinetic family drawing, a picture of the family in which every member was doing something. Then each person shared their drawings. Gloria drew a picture of the family going to church together; Ernesto's picture had everyone sitting around the dinner table. The children drew pictures of each family member acting in isolation. Esperanza drew her father at work and her mother waiting to see a doctor, and drew herself preparing dinner for her brothers. Miguel described his picture, "Mother and Father are off at work (they didn't appear in his picture) and I'm playing with Arturo. Esperanza is bothering us." Little Arturo's picture was a bit difficult to make out, probably due to his age. I saw a theme of insecurity in the children's pictures.

I asked the parents to discuss rituals and daily routines. There were discrepancies between the family culture as described in this conversation with the parents and what they had portrayed in the pictures. Gloria talked about having very little time to have family meals together and yet Ernesto drew the family having dinner together. Ernesto said he took the children to church alone and Gloria drew a picture showing her going to church with the family.

Session 3. I asked the family to describe a typical day in their home. As usual, no one took the initiative to respond. I asked Ernesto and Gloria to begin. It became apparent that they didn't know what the other was doing in the home. I pointed this out, and Gloria explained, "We work different schedules. Ernesto leaves for work before the children wake up in the morning, and he gets home right before they get home on the school bus. I leave home before the children return from school and I return home when they are already asleep."

In structural family therapy, maps and symbols are used to illustrate a family's hierarchy of authority and boundaries between members. My map of the Lopez family indicated a weak hierarchy of authority and unclear boundaries. This ran counter to the stereotype of the immigrant Hispanic families in which traditional roles of husband and wife are strongly supported.

Session 4. I wanted the parents to establish and enforce family rules and mutually support family rituals despite their work schedules. We worked on rules and routines for bedtime, homework, and getting ready for school. Contrary to the stereotype, Gloria dominated the session while Ernesto was passive. When I asked about his thoughts, he responded, "Whatever you want me to do, I will do because I love my family very much."

Gloria complained, "It should be his job as father and husband to make the rules."

Ernesto replied, "You never listen. I don't want you working crazy hours and you do it anyway."

Gloria shot back, "We never agree on anything."

Session 5. The entire family was back. I asked them to work together to draw a family crest. Esperanza tried to be the boss but the other children each fought for their own way. It was chaos. The parents failed to take charge. I encouraged Gloria and Ernesto to intervene but neither did anything. I commented on the need for leadership, and Ernesto finally talked to the children about his expectations for their behavior, "I am very upset when you cannot cooperate, and I need you to work together to complete the activity Dr. Granato has asked of us." I suggested that he get Gloria on his side.

Gloria chose this session to talk to the children about her cancer. While they had known about the cancer, she gave them more details about her treatment.

Session 6. I taught Gloria and Ernesto how to use "I messages" and "You messages." I also encouraged enforcing rules through natural and logical consequences. The children participated in brainstorming for consequences, which were ultimately determined by the parents.

Session 7. I asked Gloria and Ernesto to come in without the children again. I saw them as disengaged as a couple. Gloria made excuses, "We are so busy and barely cross paths." I commented, "Are you so busy that you can't find even a few minutes a day for each other?"

Gloria responded, "We each try to do what's best for the children." I was simply amazed, as I had observed divorced couples with stronger parental subsystems and more communication than this couple.

"I believe your schedules are a way of hiding." The startled look on Gloria's face and Ernesto's fidgeting indicated that I was on the right track.

Counselor:	Tell me about your history as a couple.
Gloria:	I don't know what to say.
Counselor:	Why don't we start with what initially attracted you to one another.
Ernesto:	We were forced to get married when Gloria found out she was pregnant.

But there was much more than this unplanned pregnancy. Gloria was crying, "My uncle raped me and I have not been able to trust men. It is so difficult to trust anyone." Gloria was 12 years old when this occurred.

Session 8. I met again with the couple.

Ernesto:	I don't understand why she never told me about the rape. Did she think that I would leave her? (He took Gloria's hand.)
Counselor:	Do you feel support from Ernesto?"
Gloria:	(Crying.) Yes, I meant to protect him. I am so sorry.
Ernesto:	I want you to know I love you no matter what.

Session 9. The children were included. Gloria and Ernesto sat next to one another. Esperanza appeared disturbed by this and tried to get Ernesto to move over and let her sit between them. Instead, Ernesto said to Esperanza, "Sit next to your brother."

I tried family sculpting. Esperanza threw a tantrum and tried to elicit support from Gloria, "Please, Mom, I love you." It looked to me as though Esperanza was losing her position of authority in the family and was trying to reestablish the alliance with her mother.

Esperanza sat in Gloria's lap and sucked her thumb. Gloria was giving in, and I commented, "Your children are scared. It is frightening for children to be in charge. Are you going to let Esperanza set the rules?" Gloria directed Esperanza to sit back in her chair.

Session 10. I asked each family member to give each other feedback on progress in the sessions. Gloria thanked Ernesto for his support. Ernesto thanked Gloria for her honesty and dedication. Ernesto spoke to the children on behalf of both parents, "We are proud of you for respecting our family rules."

Outcome

As the school counselor, I functioned as a liaison between the family system and school system. There were 10 counseling sessions, in accord with a limit set by the school district; school counselors must make a referral after 10 sessions in a school year.

I consider this case a success. I helped shore up the hierarchy of parental authority. I facilitated communication between the parents about a painful secret, a childhood rape. I also helped the parents talk to the children about Gloria's cancer. Esperanza's teachers report improvements in peer relations and better grades. Finally, Gloria followed through on my referral to a community agency for ongoing counseling.

Discussion

The Lopez family are best understood in the context of culture and religion. For example, as a Catholic, Gloria commented, "Divorce doesn't happen in our family. Divorce does not exist where we are from in Puerto Rico." For my part, although I grew up in a middle-class neighborhood on Long Island, New York, I am a first-generation Italian Catholic. I believe that my proximity to the immigrant experience helped me build rapport in this case.

I want to strongly encourage school counselors to provide family counseling. What a limited picture I would have seen had I worked with Esperanza alone!

Biographical Statement

Laura A. Granato, PhD, is assistant professor and director of the school counseling program at George Washington University. She has had seven years of experience as a school counselor in rural, suburban, and urban schools, and currently maintains a private practice with a specialization in counseling with families of children with learning disabilities and attention-deficit disorder. You can reach Laura at laura@lauragranato.com.

CHAPTER 6

The Defense Never Rests

Arthur J. Clark

Arthur J. Clark, a school psychologist at the time of this case, describes a sixth-grader's relinquishment of denial, rationalization, and blame. Ed was a difficult, resistant young man (Oppositional Defiant Disorder, DSM-IV-TR). Dr. Clark chose Adlerian, person-centered, and cognitive-behavioral approaches based on information he had gleaned from projective tests and background provided by parents and teachers.

Clark effectively explains the therapeutic process in this chapter, and discloses his rationales, doubts, and feelings as he helped Ed move from awareness to comprehension to consolidation over the course of 14 weekly sessions.

The note from the teacher read, "Please attend a meeting with me and two very anxious parents to discuss their son, Ed Reynolds (age 11), who is having problems in my class." Prior to joining the conference for Ed, I quickly checked his school records. He had moved with his family from a distant state at the start of the school year. His academic progress was inconsistent, even though his standardized test results were in the above average to superior range. He had an older sister in the eighth grade and a brother in high school. Ed's medical history was unremarkable. An unsigned note in his folder did stand out: "Extremely demanding and involved parents, especially father."

As I entered the conference, I immediately felt the tension between the classroom teacher, Mrs. White, and Ed's parents. Mr. Reynolds was questioning the quality of the school system and its lack of responsiveness to the needs of his and other children. After I made an attempt to provide another perspective on the schools, we finally started to address Ed's issues. Mrs. White stated nervously that Ed's homework was often incomplete and his grades were unsatisfactory in most areas. More importantly, she emphasized, Ed questioned the value of school assignments and expectations.

The next half hour was one of the more unpleasant that I have experienced in my many years in the public schools as a school counselor and school psychologist. Mr. Reynolds went into a lengthy and intellectualized discourse on education. He then interrogated Mrs. White about her philosophy of education, goals for teaching, professional experience, and more. My attempts to return the focus to Ed were quickly dismissed. Mrs. White, a veteran teacher who was highly respected in the school, met the challenge, but with obvious discomfort. As we had been meeting for almost an hour, the "discussion" concluded with a hurried decision for me to meet with Ed for counseling.

Conceptualization

Initially I felt relieved that the meeting was over, but I was also dissatisfied in several ways. I certainly should have been more supportive of Mrs. White. Further, I could have suggested a systems approach to working with Ed, in coordination with his teachers and his parents, or even family counseling. I consoled myself with the realization that family treatment would have been strongly rejected by the parents, who would probably think the school was shifting the blame to them.

I was uncertain how to counsel with Ed, but determined to do so as effectively as possible. A further review of Ed's school records unearthed anecdotal statements such as "He has constant excuses for his misbehavior," side by side with remarks about his high academic potential and periodic superior achievement. I also learned that Ed was interested in riding horses, swimming, and the martial arts. Additional information was gained from a discussion with Ed's history teacher, Mrs. Martin.

My immediate goal in meeting with Ed was to establish a relationship that allowed him to feel comfortable in expressing himself openly in an accepting and trusting environment. I have this relationship goal with each individual with whom I work in counseling, but I knew with Ed it would not be easy. In the initial stage of counseling I planned to use rapport- and trust-building techniques from several theories of counseling. Using person-centered therapy, I would attempt to demonstrate empathy, positive regard, and genuineness in my interactions with Ed. Using Adlerian psychology, I would emphasize equality, encouragement, and understanding the purpose of the client's behavior to strengthen our counseling alliance. And using reality therapy, I would strive to establish a climate of mutual participation and commitment, beginning by discussing interests to stimulate involvement. In theory, at least, I felt prepared.

To gain a better understanding of Ed, I decided to do a brief personality assessment using three projective techniques and my observation of Ed's behavior. I thought the projectives would also be useful in establishing rapport because of their task-centered qualities and the intrinsically interesting features of drawing and storytelling. Anticipating resistance from Ed in our initial meetings, I expected to observe his use of defense mechanisms. My task would be to recognize those defenses while providing him with support and understanding that would lessen his reliance on them in a counseling relationship, and ultimately, in his life.

Process

Just before calling Ed to my office for our initial meeting, I paused to think for a moment about what I wanted to do. My main objective was to try to establish a relationship with him, and I did not want to feel rushed about trying to do much else. Ed walked in. Before he even sat down, he asked a sarcastic question.

Ed:	Why am I here?
Counselor:	I can understand why you are concerned about that. You are probably wondering....
Ed:	When can I go back to class?
Counselor:	Well. (*Squirming in my seat, I was thinking to myself, I'm going to have a real run for my money.*) I sense that you don't feel that there is any reason for us to meet.
Ed:	When can I leave?

This was going nowhere fast, and I needed to do something.

Counselor:	You feel that you are coming along in your classes.
Ed:	I am! My work is really getting better.

As of the day before our meeting, Ed was failing in all of his academic subjects. Without this information I would have had no idea that Ed was not telling me the truth. He appeared totally convinced about his improvement in his classes. His denial was entrenched. I was determined to reflect his statements without imposing my evaluation on the truth of his words. I mistakenly hoped this would enable him to be more candid. It was time to shift to my backup strategy of discussing Ed's interests in swimming and horses. It worked, and we had a spirited talk.

As our time was drawing to a close, I decided to take advantage of Ed's good mood and at least begin the projectives. As soon as I asked Ed to draw me a picture of a person, he started in again.

Ed:	Why do I have to do this?
Counselor:	It will give me a better understanding of you. (*After saying this, I thought, Why would Ed want that?*)
Ed:	I don't have any problems!
Counselor:	You don't like it when people say that you are having difficulties in school.
Ed:	I'm sick of it. I thought for a minute that you might be different, but you're on my back like everyone else. I'm going back to class.

We were back to where we started almost 40 minutes before. After a few more minutes of my reflecting on Ed's feelings, the bell rang and Ed quickly got up and left my office. I was drained and, to say the least, discouraged. I should have followed through on the drawing. For most clients the figure drawing helps strengthen the counseling relationship. Then again, maybe I had pushed Ed too hard and I should have stayed with his interests. But if we had discussed only those activities that Ed enjoys, our session would have been superficial and I would not have learned much about Ed. And then my worst doubt: Would there be another meeting?

A week passed and I felt relieved when I saw him enter the office area; at least he had decided to show up for his appointment. I wondered about how resistant he would be in our session, and it did not take long to find out.

Ed:	I really don't have to see you if I don't want to.
Counselor:	You're pretty upset, and you don't like being told what to do.
Ed:	I am! I don't have to do anything if I don't want to.
Counselor:	You hate being bossed around.
Ed:	(*A long silence.*) I'm tired and I want to go back to class.

Just when I thought for a moment we were coming together, Ed wants to end it. Acknowledging Ed's fatigue, I attempted to stimulate discussion around the theme of feelings of coercion; Ed would have none of it. I feared our second session was quickly coming to an end and I still did not have much of an understanding of Ed. I decided to try the projectives again.

Counselor:	I can see that you are pretty tired, but we need to complete a few tasks.
Ed:	What do you mean "tasks"?
Counselor:	Well, they are kinds of evaluations for self-understanding.
Ed:	I don't need any self-understanding.
Counselor:	What I mean is that you are struggling in school and this may help in understanding why.

For a few minutes we went on like this, and Ed finally yielded, mainly, I think, to stop me from explaining further. Once Ed began his figure drawing, he quickly became interested in the activity. He also showed reasonable effort and cooperation on the sentence completion and early recollections. Over the years, I have observed many resistant clients let down their guard after accepting and becoming involved in completing projectives.

Projective techniques are criticized for their questionable psychometric qualities: only moderate levels of validity and reliability, lack of representative norms, and imprecise scoring systems. Yet, even with these limitations, I find the projectives highly revealing of a client's personality dynamics, and they have become an integral part of the counseling process for many individuals with whom I work. I try to avoid speculative interpretations and attempt to generate reasonable inferences or hypotheses from multiple client responses on the projective instruments.

Ed's drawing was revealing; he depicted a person with arms outstretched, no hands, near the top of the page. Arms reaching into the environment suggests a need for affection and acceptance, and placement high on the page indicates uncertainty and lack of support in the environment. Omission of hands is related to feelings of inadequacy. From this, I developed hypotheses about Ed's low self-esteem and his need to be accepted by others in a supportive and caring environment—aspects of Ed's personality that he simply did not demonstrate in his counseling sessions.

As it is with many clients, Ed's sentence completion was illuminating, especially in identifying his use of defense mechanisms. Denial was indicated when he wrote, "I regret...nothing" and "I failed...nothing." His sentence "My father...is nice" was contradicted in a later completion, "I wish...my father would get off my back." Ed's use of rationalization was apparent when he wrote, "I failed...history because of my dumb teacher" and "Other kids...get me in trouble." His opinion of the formal learning process was summarized with, "School...is a waste of time."

The use of early recollections as a projective technique is derived from the work of Alfred Adler. The client is asked to recall at least three memories from a period before 8 years of age. Each memory must be visualized in a single, specific event. Ed related his first memory in a subdued tone.

Ed: I spilled milk on the kitchen floor, and my father was
                        standing over me as I cleaned it up.

Ed's second memory also included his father:

Ed: I was learning to ride my bicycle, and my father was
                        teaching me. He said that he would hold on to me, but he
                        let go and I fell.

A third memory depicted Ed at his birthday party:

Ed: I had a nice birthday cake, but only two kids were at my
                        party. There was a lot of stuff to eat, but not enough kids
                        were there.

With each of his memories I asked Ed how he felt, and he replied, "Stupid and mad." Ed's early recollections suggested his sense of incompetence in an unkind environment. His lack of support from people, particularly in his dealings with his father, was evident. His feelings were a mix of hostility and disappointment.

With only a few minutes left in our session, I asked Ed about several of his responses on the sentence completion. He wanted no part of this, and he insisted on going back to his class. With his departure I felt relief but also hope, as now I had a better understanding of Ed.

Between counseling sessions, I assessed Ed's projectives and reflected on the direction I should take and even wondered if we should continue to meet. However, I was challenged in two ways by Ed: I felt that I could work with him effectively, and I was intrigued by his defenses. After a discussion with Ed's teachers and a telephone conversation with his mother, I agreed to continue our weekly sessions.

In my next meeting with Ed, I immediately questioned my decision to continue counseling. He was hostile and sarcastic for the major part of our time together. Relentlessly he questioned the value and need for our sessions. At the same time, Ed continued to deny any problems of his own, stating again and again that he was improving in his school subjects, while criticizing his teachers for their incompetence and lack of understanding.

There were times when Ed was blasting his teachers that his statements seemed at least plausible, especially when he gave examples to support his position. Ed recounted a complaint about his history class.

Ed:The book is so stupid. I'm only in the sixth grade and the book is written for high school kids.

Counselor:(*Knowing something about the text and the teacher.*) It sounds like the book is difficult, but Mrs. Martin clarifies a lot of it in class.

What I thought was a sensible statement became lost as Ed continued to employ the defense of rationalization.

Ed:You really don't know what you are talking about. Have you ever read the book? She even said in class that the book is too hard. You can't even understand half of what she says because so many kids fool around in her class.

Well, I knew that Mrs. Martin was having difficulty with discipline in some of her classes. She told me that the book was excessively demanding. Each of Ed's assertions had a sufficient degree of truth to give credibility to his position. He also expressed himself with such conviction that attempting to determine the degree of validity of his statements was a challenge, to say the least. As I weighed his responses, what helped me the most was the understanding I had gained from the projectives that Ed employs denial, rationalization, and perhaps, displacement. Secondly, I knew that in any defense there must be an element of plausibility or it would have no deception value.

Our session ended and again I felt discouraged; we had made no real progress in our meeting. I needed to forget about Ed, and I went to see what was in my mailbox. Mrs. Martin had written me a note: "Ed's behavior has deteriorated even further. Now he does absolutely nothing in my class." She was kind to leave out what was implied, "since he began meeting with you." Now the pressure would be increasing from Ed's teachers for him to show some improvement in his behavior.

My discouragement suddenly ended with my fourth session with Ed. He had received a high grade on a class assignment and was delighted to tell me about it. I reflected his pleasure in the accomplishment, and I thought that a turning point had been made in our relationship. It seemed timely for me to disclose how I had also struggled in school with inconsistent progress, but Ed was unimpressed with this and he offered no indication that he cared about my educational history or, even worse, about me. He seemed to deny or ignore the intimacy my words offered, as though his self-preoccupation prevented him from being affected by another person's experiences. Feeling resentful toward Ed, I shifted the topic from myself back to his good grade in class. Once again, Ed spoke with satisfaction about his work. At that moment, even though I apparently mattered little to him, I was able to muster concern for him out of my belief in the intrinsic value and worth of people.

Our next session provided a new low point in our relationship. Ed began in a caustic tone: "You haven't helped me at all and my parents agree with me on this." Although I have been accused of not being helpful from time to time by clients, this occasion was more painful than usual because of the strong effort I had extended on Ed's behalf, and my supposed expertise in working with resistant clients. My participant–observer stance held up long enough for me to state, "Everyone has their preferences." But inside I felt like telling Ed to get out of my office and go tell his parents to find some other counselor to put up with his obnoxious and self-centered behavior. After our session, I engaged in some self-reflection on the topic of countertransference: Why did Ed upset me this way?

Even more intriguing to me were Ed's unyielding mechanisms of defense. How could I continue to be a threat to this young person after a number of weeks of offering him understanding, respect, encouragement, and a reasonable degree of genuineness? What is the tenacity of Ed's defenses that compels him to maintain his guardedness in front of a middle-aged man who has clearly demonstrated that he is on his side? The thought of terminating with Ed started to take on a new appeal.

One of the difficulties in working in the schools is that when counseling fails the client remains on the premises as a constant reminder to the counselor and to all others present. Of course, the counselor, using his or her defenses, can rationalize either that the client expended no effort in the sessions or was not ready to change. I did, however, have to face the fact that unless we established some degree of mutual trust there would be little sense in continuing to meet.

As it was time for our sixth session, I was hoping that Ed would be absent or late for his appointment. Right on time, Ed began, "I've decided that coming here is not so bad because it gets my father off my back some." What a relief this was for me. For the first time in several sessions Ed gave me an indication that the counseling process held some promise of progress. I very much wanted to be precise and accurate in my response to Ed.

Counselor:	You seem really determined. It's important for you to be able to make up your own mind.
Ed:	Yeah, I get sick of people telling me what to do. My father thinks that he knows everything.
Counselor:	You resent it that your opinion is not worth much, especially when you are with your father.
Ed:	He thinks that I am stupid, and so do a lot of other people.

Ed was making statements that were rich in therapeutic potential. I was gratified that we had reached this point, and I wanted to be sure that we effectively processed what he expressed. In my notes, I wrote verbatim some of his statements. As Ed continued, two related themes emerged: feeling coerced and feeling intellectually inferior. This session with Ed was by far the most satisfying for me. As he confided in me, I felt relieved that a relationship had finally begun to take hold, and my doubts gave way to more confidence in my strategies and interventions. I felt that continuing to provide Ed with understanding and acceptance was essential in reducing his guardedness and developing trust. It was more than satisfying for me to have this assumption confirmed by his response to me in this session. I now had to consider where to proceed in the middle stage in the counseling process.

It was time for me to become more active and to share with Ed what I had learned about him in our six weeks together. In particular, I wanted to focus on Ed's self-defeating and maladaptive thoughts. The work of the cognitive-behavioral therapists, including Albert Ellis, Aaron Beck, and Donald Meichenbaum, would be central in my efforts. I also wanted to challenge contradictions in Ed's behavior, but in a way that would not jeopardize our counseling relationship. Confrontation, a gestalt intervention, would be crucial to me in this attempt.

At our seventh session the focus shifted to Ed's thinking or cognitions, as we entered what I refer to as the integration stage of counseling. As Ed talked about feeling inadequate in school, I confronted him in a supportive tone, "You feel that you can't do that well in the class, but you also tell me that you don't do any of the homework." If I had said this to Ed a few weeks before, he would have responded with anger and indignation. Instead Ed replied in a more resigned way, "Sometimes I'm just a lot of talk." His sense of despair prompted me to disclose how I personally had experienced many difficulties in school, much as I had told him several weeks before. This time he seemed encouraged by my words.

Ed's contradictory behavior was most apparent in his classroom performance. He constantly spoke (although with diminished intensity) about resenting being told what to do, but he also expressed discouragement about feeling "stupid." In a reassuring tone I attempted to relate two prominent and contradictory assumptions Ed had made.

Counselor:	You talk a lot about how important it is for you to make decisions for yourself and that you hate being told what to do. (If there was one conviction of Ed's that he and I had established, this was it.)
Ed:	So?
Counselor:	Well, I'm trying to figure it out too. You always want to get your own way, but you also don't like being seen as not very smart.

My attempt to juxtapose Ed's contradictory positions began to make sense to him. If Ed insisted on getting his own way all the time, did this mean he was not being very smart? I was not fully sure where we might go with this, but a softening of either assumption would be a positive change. Ed then began a direct appeal to me.

Ed:	I'm not really dumb, you know. A lot of times I fake it so that I get my own way.
Counselor:	(*I decided to really open it up.*) So often Ed, you blame other people for things when it really is more your own fault.
Ed:	(*After a lengthy silence.*) I'm taking a hard look at this. I do have ways to get around things. I just want to be somebody. . . . I'm a nobody.

Ed was expressing such significant feelings that I had a difficult time responding in effective ways. Staying with what seemed to be working, I continued to traverse the web of Ed's contradictory behavior. Together Ed and I openly explored the numerous inconsistencies in his young existence, and there were many. We were progressing, but I felt that we still were not reaching Ed's more fundamental premises about life, because he continued to engage defense mechanisms when he felt pressured.

Our next session began with what appeared to be a setback, when Ed made statements about topics that I thought we had already worked through: "School really doesn't matter," "I really don't care about anything around here." In a supportive yet firm way I challenged Ed's statements, using cognitive restructuring.

Counselor: You are giving up any real chance to get anywhere in the future by not trying in school. Why not do what you can about making things better by controlling what you can?

I spoke with deep conviction in my voice because I touched on a topic that has meaning for me, and I was clearly reaching Ed. As I spoke, he was looking at me with an intensity that I had never seen before.

Counselor: If you want to be somebody in life, you need to put an effort into it. You can't just wish for things to happen and blame other people when they don't work out.

As I went on, I became aware that I had to let Ed respond. I did not want to lose the impact that I seemed to be making on him. With my pause, Ed reacted in a subdued statement, "I look for excuses all the time, rather than do more on my own." This jumped out at me! I asked him to repeat exactly what he had said, so I could write it down in my notes. As Ed spoke the words again, I was aware of the "therapeutic moment" and wished to take full advantage of it.

Counselor: Ed, you said something that is not easy to say; go on.
Ed: For a long time I've been thinking about how I try to blame everyone else for my problems, rather than blame myself.

This induced a lengthy silence (for me, anything over one minute is lengthy). Ed did not look like he was going to speak but I told myself to be quiet. Finally, Ed spoke: "I'm tired. I really don't want to talk about this much more."

This threw me. Just when I was excited about a breakthrough that could spark a behavior change, Ed said he was tired. What about the therapeutic moment? I certainly wanted to continue, but wondered if I should push Ed when he had expressed so much and now wanted to stop. As it turned out, we did shift to another topic, and although we returned repeatedly to the control theme in our sessions, Ed never again expressed the depth of awareness that he had reached in this encounter.

In our tenth session, Ed began by complaining about how unfair one of his teachers was in her grading. As Ed went on, I thought back on our recent meetings where he appeared to fully realize how he defended himself while avoiding responsibility for his actions. This realization now seemed lost on Ed. I went on to challenge his perceptions through cognitive restructuring, much as I had done in our last session. During our next two meetings the themes of Ed's acceptance of responsibility and avoidance of blaming other people for his problems were emphasized. Ed was particularly pleased when I informed him that his teacher, Mrs. White, told me that he had started to improve in his work and that he was now "enjoyable to have in class."

Only once during this period did we discuss what I thought was a central conflict in his life: Ed's relationship with his father. At one point in an earlier session, he stated that his father liked it when Ed did "lousy" in school. I confronted Ed with my observation that his father seemed interested in how Ed did in school, and said I did not understand his statement. Perhaps I had cut off consideration of Ed's perception at that time, because he did not mention it again for several weeks. This time, when Ed spoke about how his father really did not care about how well he performed academically, I offered an interpretation: "Could it be that you used to do poorly because of your dad's dislike of school that you have heard so much about?" When I said this it seemed rather implausible and Ed did not want to discuss the topic further.

We did not go beyond this attempt to clarify Ed's relationship with his father. It was evident all along that Ed felt both resentment and apprehension toward his father. I thought about Ed's early recollection of his dad standing over him after Ed spilled his milk. Perhaps if Ed had indicated more interest, we would have pursued this further. Ed seemed to be progressing in other ways, so I did not attempt further interpretations to explore developmental conflicts. In retrospect, I am aware that Ed's relationship with his father required further clarification.

Outcome

The main accomplishments of counseling with Ed were his increasingly accurate and integrated thoughts that developed over twelve sessions. In the final stage of counseling Ed discussed changes in his belief systems with satisfaction: "I still try to blame other people when things go wrong, but I'm getting better at owning up to things." I offered Ed frequent encouragement by emphasizing his control, effort, and capabilities. In particular, I stressed growth in his adaptive behavior and the diminished power of his defense mechanisms: "You are more honest with yourself" (less denial), "You face up to things better now" (less rationalization), and "It's hard, but now you blame other people a lot less when things don't work out" (less displacement).

Meaningful change, however, must be manifested in productive actions. Ed's negative self-evaluation and defense mechanisms were well established, and they did not yield easily to more productive patterns. We used cognitive-behavioral techniques to facilitate purposeful change. Ed tried the Adlerian technique of catching himself each time he began to talk about a negative attribute ("I'm stupid—I must always get my own way"), or a defense (denial, rationalization, and displacement were combined under avoiding responsibility). One week Ed carried a small notebook in his pocket and recorded his behavior. Ed caught himself using such negative talk 19 times. With a decline in frequency of such behaviors over a few weeks, Ed felt a further sense of accomplishment.

My time with Ed was drawing to a close, and we began to talk about terminating counseling in our fourteenth meeting. I felt very satisfied about our work together, especially since I had come so close to giving up early in our sessions.

In a meeting with Ed's parents and his teachers near the end of the school year, I eagerly anticipated a discussion in which I expected to receive credit for my good work with Ed. After a review of the academic and social progress that Ed had made, it was time for Ed's father to speak: "I think that most of the improvement with Ed came about because my wife and I enrolled him in a karate class." Somehow it all didn't seem very fair.

Discussion

It is sometimes difficult in the midst of the counseling process to fully appraise the progress of a case. Only after moving through the stages of the counseling process is it possible to accurately assess outcomes. Of course, the most important outcome is how the client progresses in his or her life after counseling concludes. Looking back in my counseling with Ed, I can see that I made some mistakes and avoided others. I can point to many positive elements in the growth of our relationship. In writing about Ed, I chose to present a case in which the outcome was successful rather than one that was less rewarding. I try to learn from my experience and to enjoy the more positive outcomes.

Several times I considered terminating with Ed, particularly early in our relationship. I thought that we were not progressing and would not be able to establish a counseling relationship. Sometimes I become impatient and expect progress, forgetting that the counseling process occurs in irregular gains, delays, and reversals. I also thought about terminating because I was being worn down by Ed's obstinacy and general unpleasantness. If I had allowed termination to occur, both Ed and I would have missed an opportunity to grow.

I find that I need to remind myself that the counseling process is often enhanced by working with the larger system. Reflecting on my first conference with Ed's teacher and parents, I suspect that if I had been more assertive (actually courageous) in my support of Mrs. White, I might have struck a more advantageous service arrangement. For example, working in consultation with Ed's teachers or starting family counseling should have at least been discussed. I made no attempt to establish a team approach, which frequently has more potential for success. Instead, I settled for expecting positive behavior change to occur only through individual counseling.

At different times I felt pressure from Ed's teachers and parents to achieve a quicker behavior change. As a result, I attempted to force the counseling process in several instances by intervening excessively and prematurely. For example, I offered a self-disclosure (about my failures in school) that was too intimate before Ed and I had established our counseling relationship. Even worse, I blamed Ed when this intervention didn't work. Most of the time, I was able to trust the counseling process and remain solidly focused on the relationship.

The least effective intervention with Ed was interpretation. He resisted my efforts to relate his conflicted feelings to his developmental experiences. I was not sure if the strength of Ed's feelings had subsided or if he was defending with restricted affect. Another possibility is that I did not employ interpretation effectively. We had little success in linking Ed's past to his current functioning. Since my time with Ed, I have attempted to improve my understanding of interpretation in the counseling process, especially in working with young clients. This effort remains unfinished for me, but I am intrigued by it.

The conceptualization of the counseling process into three stages provides me with a general direction for client progress. This does not mean that a hypothetical stage is clearly apparent or that the process is irreversible. The sequence of stages, however, does affect the timing of strategies and interventions within each stage. For example, the positive impact of cognitive restructuring depended on my previous challenge of Ed's contradictory behavior through confrontation.

Modifying a client's defenses in a specific sequence within the three stages of counseling facilitates an understanding of how change occurs. In the initial stage Ed became aware that he was experiencing defensive feelings. He increased his comprehension of how and why he engaged defenses in the integration stage. And in the final stage of counseling Ed assumed a more adaptive manner of functioning. Somehow the stages never seem this neat and tidy during the counseling experience, but looking back, one can see that the process of change occurs in a sequential way.

The operation of a client's defense mechanisms has fascinated me for a long time. Over the years, I have learned that several strategies are not beneficial, and I avoid using them. The to-be-avoided list in handling defenses in counseling includes tolerating, disputing, and attacking. Tolerating defense mechanisms may be necessary in the beginning of a relationship, but it is unrealistic to expect enduring patterns to change in an emotionally comfortable climate. Examining contradictions and distortions that are inherent in defenses also allows for their cognitive foundations to be clarified. Although in the initial stage of counseling with Ed I was tolerant as he exhibited defenses, I shifted to a more challenging stance in the middle stage and confronted his contradictory behavior. Disputing, in the form of bickering or arguing with a client over the validity or legitimacy of his or her defenses invariably results in a more urgent and intense display of the mechanisms. Attacking or stripping defenses makes a client feel exposed and vulnerable: he or she may fall apart or mount even stronger defenses.

Ed came by the school to visit last year. After he told me that he was doing well, he said, "I don't know how you put up with me. I used to blame my parents, my teachers, and everyone else for my problems except me." It was so good to see Ed again.

Reference

American Psychiatric Association. (2000). *Diagnostic and statistical manual of mental disorders: DSM-IV-TR* (4th ed., text revision). Washington, DC: Author.

Biographical Statement

Arthur J. Clark, EdD, is associate professor and coordinator of the counseling and development program at St. Lawrence University in Canton, New York. In working with children, Arthur has been employed as a school counselor, director of guidance, and school psychologist. He is the author of *Defense Mechanisms in the Counseling Process* (Sage, 1998). You can reach Arthur at aclark@mail.stlawu.edu.

CHAPTER 7

Mandy: Out in the World

Barbara Herlihy

Barbara Herlihy presents the case of an 11-year-old girl who comes to her already burdened with a severe diagnosis: Schizoid Personality Disorder (*DSM-IV-TR*). Herlihy uses a child-centered approach in individual counseling with occasional family interventions. The medium of music becomes an important way of connecting with this unusual child.

Herlihy deals with two basic therapeutic issues. First, Mandy is emotionally withdrawn from family and peers and seems to have always been so. She seems quite content when alone in her bedroom playing the flute. Does the therapist have a right to tamper with Mandy's chosen approach to life? If we can agree that it is appropriate to modify pernicious behavior in another person, does it follow that it is desirable, or possible, to change a personality trait? Second, when Herlihy's work with Mandy bogs down, her impulse is to refer Mandy out to someone, anyone, with more experience in treating personality disorders! Do such impulses emanate from a keen awareness of professional ethics or from a hidden source of resistance within the therapist? We "overhear" a seasoned therapist wrestle with these issues.

W hen 11-year old Mandy walked into my office, I was struck by her pale, almost ghostly appearance. She was tall for her age and very thin. Her long, straight hair was ash blonde, and her face was so pale that I wondered whether she was allergic to the sun. At her mother's prompting, she piped a reedy and barely audible hello. My first impression, one that would mislead me for some time, was of a child who was not only wraithlike but very fragile.

My contact with Mandy was preceded by a phone call from Donna Alvarez, her middle school counselor. Donna occasionally referred to me, in my private practice, a child whose counseling needs went beyond what she could provide in the school setting. She told me that Mandy's mother, Ann, had requested a referral. She had provided a list of referral sources, and Ann had selected me and asked Donna to call me and share background information. Donna stated that she had mailed me a signed release of information form. She described Mandy as a loner who had no close friends and who always ate lunch alone in a corner of the school cafeteria. She had no record of discipline problems at school and had been absent on several occasions for extended periods of time. Her grades were above average: mostly B's, a few C's, and an occasional A. She had performed well enough on the Cognitive Abilities Tests (CogAT) to be eligible for placement in the gifted and talented program but had lacked the needed grades and teacher recommendation.

Based on the information from Donna, I had formed a tentative picture of Mandy as extremely shy and possibly school phobic. During my initial meeting with Mandy and Ann, I gained no information from Mandy that would add to the picture. Despite my best efforts to include Mandy, Ann did all the talking.

Ann's concern about Mandy was deep and abiding. As she described their home life, it became apparent that Mandy was a loner within the family as well as at school. Mandy's typical after-school routine was to close herself in her bedroom and do her homework until dinnertime, emerging only for the meal with the family. After dinner, she would retreat to her room to finish her studying, practice her flute, or listen to music until she went to sleep. She rarely went outdoors, and never invited a friend to the house. Occasionally, she would receive a phone call from a schoolmate asking for help with a homework assignment. Mandy willingly gave the help but didn't linger on the phone to socialize. Ann's frustration was evident when she stated, "Mandy doesn't communicate with us. I don't know how she feels, what she thinks. I can't even get her to tell me what she'd like for dinner!"

As Ann continued to relate various anecdotes, a pattern was emerging. She would have extended periods of being patient, encouraging, and protective of Mandy. Then she would snap in frustration, yell at her daughter, and seek outside help. I imagined that Mandy knew the pattern well and didn't trust the patient and supportive mother, and that each of Ann's outbursts was driving her further into herself. It seemed like Ann needed to detach from her daughter; this was an easy prescription to give but a very difficult one to follow for a parent who was so intensely concerned.

Ann's further comments revealed that the problem was long-standing. Over the past three years, she had taken Mandy to one psychologist and two psychiatrists. Mandy had been hospitalized twice. At this point, I requested and received permission to contact the previous therapists. Then, speaking directly to Mandy in Ann's presence, I repeated my explanation of confidentiality. I asked Ann to give me some time to get to know Mandy. Ann gave her daughter a hug, to which Mandy responded as limply as a rag doll, and left the room.

Mandy and I had about 15 minutes together in the remainder of the first session. She spent most of the time with her head bowed. School was "OK," she "didn't know" how she felt about coming to see me, and my open-ended questions were met with a shrug. I was not surprised by her reluctance to communicate with me. I simply attempted to provide a safe climate and to convey both verbally and through my body language a calm acceptance. Since her mother crowded her with intensity, she needed to feel my respect for her personal space. She said "OK" to my invitation to return the next week, although I believed she was bowing to her mother's wishes rather than expressing her own desires.

Conceptualization

As I gathered information from the other helping professionals who had worked with Mandy, it became apparent that her condition was difficult to diagnose. The psychologist, whom Mandy had seen when she was eight, had tentatively made a diagnosis of Avoidant Disorder of Childhood with an accompanying anxiety disorder, based on her shrinking from contact with people, her inarticulate and often mute response in the therapeutic setting, and reported impaired social functioning in peer relationships. He also noted that therapy had not been deemed effective.

The psychiatrist whom Mandy had seen two years ago sent his records. He had recommended hospitalization and had continued as her primary therapist during her inpatient treatment. He had diagnosed Mandy as schizophrenic. She had told him that she "saw another face in the mirror," and he had also noted her flat affect, impaired interpersonal functioning, social withdrawal, and emotional detachment. He had prescribed an antipsychotic medication but noted that "its only effect was to make her sleepy." Mandy had been minimally compliant with the 21-day treatment program.

The other psychiatrist, who had worked with Mandy 10 months ago, called me when he received my request for information. He related that he had initially made a diagnosis of Schizotypal Personality Disorder but later changed it to Schizoid Personality Disorder. He, too, had recommended hospitalization, and Mandy's parents had complied. Again, as with the previous psychiatrist, he had found no medication to have a positive effect. Her hospital stay had been brief. When Mandy's parents came to visit, she cried and begged to be taken home. Her parents withdrew her from the hospital after six days.

I was left with a variety of possible diagnoses, all sharing similar characteristics. The diagnostic criteria for Schizoid Personality Disorder seemed to come closest to describing Mandy. According to the *DSM-IV-TR*, a person with this disorder neither desires nor enjoys close relationships, including being part of a family, almost always chooses solitary activities, rarely if ever appears to experience strong emotions, has no close friends or confidants, and displays constricted affect.

Although this diagnosis seemed possibly appropriate, I felt reluctant to consider it. I didn't *want* it to be correct. My experience with personality disorders, aside from my clinical training, was rather limited. The vast majority of my clients in private practice, adults and children alike, came to me with a keen interest in self-exploration and the capability of translating awareness into behavioral change. Therefore, improvements were often rewarding for them and me. My impression of personality-disordered individuals is that their world view and subsequent behavioral patterns have become so entrenched that they may not desire change. They often enter counseling only because their loved ones are troubled by their symptoms. This seemed to be the case with Mandy; her mother sought help for her, and Mandy seemed to acquiesce in a resigned way.

The prognosis for this disorder is quite limiting. The *DSM-IV-TR* states that males are usually incapable of dating and rarely marry, while females may passively accept courtship and marry. Social relations remain severely constricted, while occupational functioning may be impaired except in work conditions of social isolation. This seemed such a bleak outlook for an 11-year-old child. Nonetheless, it was my initial, tentative diagnosis.

Process

As we began our second session, Mandy sat with her head bowed, her hands in her lap. She responded with silence, a shrug, or "I don't know" to my attempts to make contact. We were sliding into a question-and-answer session that was going nowhere. I became increasingly aware of an anxious knot in my stomach. The knot reminded me of an interminable hour I had endured during my practicum experience at the master's level. At that time my client was a reluctant 9- or 10-year-old boy who refused to verbalize. I watched the tape spin around on the recorder and knew that my professor was not going to be impressed with a tape full of silence. I filled the tape with the sound of my voice, wondering if I was saying the right thing, thinking the hour would never end. I had gotten a terrible grade on that performance and didn't need to repeat it here and now.

Since talk therapy was proving unproductive, I changed strategies. Mandy seemed relieved to be offered some manipulatives. She would draw or use materials when given a specific suggestion, although she initiated nothing on her own. At the end of the hour, when we were both engaged in putting things away, I asked her again how she felt about coming to see me. When she responded with a shrug, I offered, "I'm trying to imagine how I would feel if I were 11 years old and my mother kept dragging me around to see counselors." As I expressed my feelings, Mandy stopped her tidying-up activities, and for the first time looked straight at me. I finished by saying, "So, I don't know whether I'd want to come back." After a pause, Mandy said, "I want to come back." I felt encouraged as she left. She had made one definitive statement, and it was a beginning.

As our third session progressed, my hopes began to fade. Once again, Mandy was compliant with suggestions as we sat together in the play area, but she just seemed to be going through the motions. I couldn't find a way to connect with her at any meaningful level. Several strategies, including art activities, a sand tray, various games, and companionable silence, were met with passive acquiescence.

At one point Mandy brushed back her long hair and I caught sight of her earrings. I commented on how pretty I thought they were, and how unusual. Then, since the thought occurred to me, I went on to tell her that my best friend had a daughter who was about to have her 13th birthday. I wanted to get her a small gift, and I knew her ears were pierced like Mandy's and that she also enjoyed wearing unusual earrings. Did Mandy have any advice that might help me with my shopping? To my surprise, she had a great deal to say. She described at length the styles that were popular with girls her age, what stores would have the best selection, and so forth. I was genuinely grateful for the help, told her so, and was rewarded with a shy smile. In that moment, we had contact with each other. We had connected, but the contact was not sustained. For the remainder of the session, Mandy reverted to passivity when I failed to initiate a direction. She seemed to be lost deep inside herself. I wasn't sure she was even aware of my presence.

With Mandy's agreement, our fourth session was a family session. My hope was to gain some insights by observing the family dynamics. Mandy's father, Brad, entered my office first and sat on the sofa. As Mandy followed and sat down next to him, he draped his arm behind her over the sofa, his fingers barely touching her shoulder. Ann and Mandy's 15-year-old brother Michael took individual chairs, while her baby sister, a toddler, made straight for the toys I had placed on the floor.

Ann dominated the conversation. Brad mostly listened, although he spoke clearly and assertively when addressed directly. Michael, an average student who was very involved in athletics, was eager to be heard. He was concerned about fairness issues within the family, such as the division of household chores and whether he could drive the family car when he turned 16. As we explored such topics, I was able to suggest to Ann that perhaps she was exhausted from taking charge of so much within the family. It appeared that she was taking responsibility for all the decisions on dividing the chores, determining the allowances, and enforcing the rules. Not only did this seem to be a heavy burden for her, but it wasn't doing the others any good. If she continued to take responsibility for them, they wouldn't learn to take responsibility for themselves. She seemed grateful for the suggestion, and the session began to focus on strategies for shared decision making in which Mandy, her brother, and her father could make some choices and be accountable for them.

As the session drew to a close, I thought it had been rather productive. If Ann could ease off on her intense efforts to "fix" Mandy and force her to join in with the family, perhaps Mandy would move into the space that was created. The unspoken dynamics of the family's interactions, however, interested me more than their words. The toddler told the family story at a nonverbal level. Throughout the session, when she needed help with something like putting her shoe back on or putting a toy together, she went to her mother. When she wanted attention, she came to her brother, her parents, or me. When she just wanted to be held, she went to Brad. In the entire hour she never approached Mandy.

Mandy and I had two more individual sessions, neither of which yielded any discernible progress. I began to question my competence and brought Mandy's case to my consultation group. Without giving away Mandy's identity, I described my client, the counseling process, and my frustrations. I wondered aloud whether I should consider referring Mandy to someone with more expertise. One of the group members asked me, "Who, besides Mandy, frustrates you?" "Her mother," I replied.

"She goes through periods of being patient, protective, supportive, and encouraging. Then when Mandy doesn't change, she throws up her hands and takes Mandy out to an expert to be fixed." I felt a rueful smile form on my face. "Aha," I said. "Let me own that. *I* have been patient, supportive, protective, and encouraging. Now that *I* see no change, I'm considering sending her off to an expert." I decided, for now, to persevere.

Ann, obviously upset, followed Mandy into my office at the beginning of the seventh session. "You two need to talk about Mandy's report card," she declared, waving it in her hand. Mandy had gotten an F for the marking period in language arts. It was the first time she had ever received a failing grade. Ann explained that the major grade for the marking period had been based on a speech that the students had to give in front of the class. Mandy had refused to do it. She had stayed home from school on the last three days when she might have been called on to give her speech.

After Ann left the room, I said, "I remember that my parents were upset, too, the first time I got an F. Do you want to talk about it?" Mandy shrugged. By now, I understood that a shrug meant the topic could be explored. When Mandy didn't want to pursue a subject, she would shut down with bowed head and frozen posture. Working with a set of drawings of faces (smiling, neutral, frowning, sad, and so on), Mandy conveyed that she believed she had made the right choice. Although getting good grades was important to her, she could not and would not stand before the class, make a speech, and stand up there while it was critiqued. Mandy had made the choice and accepted the consequences, although it made her sad that her mother was angry.

I glanced at the report card her mother had placed in my hand, and noticed that Mandy had received an A+ in music. When I asked about that, Mandy smiled the broadest smile I had yet seen. She loved music and played the flute. When I asked if she would bring her flute next time and play for me, she smiled again.

Thus, it was in our eighth session that I found an entree into Mandy's emotional world. She arrived with her flute and immediately unpacked the instrument. At my invitation she began to play. As I listened, at first I was amazed at her technical proficiency. Then, I sat back and let the music affect me. Mandy had selected Pachelbel's Canon in D, a mournful, evocative piece. When she finished, there were tears brimming in my eyes. I said, "I felt so sad listening to that." Mandy looked mutely at me, and I saw that her eyes were glistening too. I added, "Sometimes I think music expresses feelings much better than words ever could." Mandy nodded in agreement. We had a focus for our session—sadness. And I had learned to communicate with Mandy by indirection.

As we worked with various materials, I discovered that it made her sad when her family worried about her. On the other hand, she didn't want to change to make them happy. When she drew a picture of her family as her parents would like it to be, she drew the five of them sitting on a sofa in front of a television. When she drew the family as she wanted it, she drew her mother in the kitchen, her father in front of the TV, her brother behind the wheel of a car, her baby sister asleep, and herself alone in her room playing the flute.

Our next two sessions followed the same format. Mandy played her flute, and we focused on the feelings the music had expressed. It seemed clear to me that we had developed a working relationship, within the limits of Mandy's expressiveness. I was tempted to kick myself, just a bit, for not making use of the flute sooner. The information about her love of music had been there from the beginning.

Despite these inroads, in Mandy's larger world nothing changed. I touched base with Donna Alvarez, her school counselor. Since I had begun working with Mandy, spring had come. Now Donna saw Mandy at lunchtime, eating her bag lunch alone on the grass outside the building. She reported that Mandy continued to go through her days essentially alone. At home Mandy continued to retreat into her room.

It was time for me to reflect on the goals of counseling. Whose goals were to be met? What Mandy's parents wanted was clear. They wanted her to join with the family and to have a "normal" social life with friends and activities. What did Mandy want? She had given me some clues. She now looked forward to our sessions and seemed to enjoy spending time with one person who would let her express herself in her own way. She wanted to please her parents. However, she didn't seem to want to make the kinds of changes that would accomplish that. Was she unable to connect with others as a result of her disorder? Was she able but lacking in social skills? Or was she truly content to be as she was? What was in Mandy's best interests? It was time to get clarification from Mandy.

I was looking for an opportunity to raise the question, and I managed to create one in our next session. It began, as usual, with Mandy playing a selection on her flute. It was a piece I didn't recognize. When I asked about it, Mandy told me that the composer was someone whose music had been unappreciated while he was alive. I commented that it must have been hard for him, knowing the kind of music he wanted to create but also knowing that others didn't want to hear it. I suggested that, perhaps in some ways, that composer's situation was like her own. He, too, was out of synch with the way other people wanted him to be. She gave me a curious glance.

I went on to say, "Mandy, you are *of* this world—you've been born into it and you are alive. But I get the impression that you live very little *in* this world, among its people. You seem quite content to be by yourself. And that's OK, if it's what you want and it doesn't bother you to be alone a lot. What happens, though, is that it seems to bother other people. It causes problems for your teachers, who have to give you lower grades when you don't participate in group activities or speak in front of the class. Possibly, it bothers people who'd like to be your friend when you don't reach out to them, and they drift away. And it bothers your parents when you don't join with the family."

I paused to gather my thoughts, and was aware as I did so that Mandy was staring straight at me, her brow furrowed in concentration. Never had I seen her look so intense. I waited. Perhaps two minutes passed. Then, with a decisive nod of her head, Mandy said, "OK." She immediately got up, went to the drawing table and picked up a sketch she had started last week. She was drawing a jazz ensemble. The faces and figures of the musicians were roughly sketched, but their instruments were carefully and precisely drawn. She worked on it, silently and with great concentration, for the rest of the hour.

After Mandy left my office, I was left to ponder that brief period of intense concentration. I thought something had happened, but I wasn't sure what. Was I creating a "significant moment" out of nothing more than a furrowed brow, a nod, and a simple "OK"?

The answer began to emerge a week later, when Ann called to say she had to work late and needed to reschedule Mandy's session. She reported that Mandy had come out of her room for a couple of hours twice during the week and had watched TV with the family. She had even volunteered to go with her brother (who now had his driver's license) when he ran some errands on Saturday.

Since we were unable to reschedule the appointment, I didn't see Mandy until the following week. Mandy came in and played the flute, but this time she had an agenda of her own. She wanted to ask her music teacher for private tutoring after school and wasn't quite sure how to go about it. We strategized together about how she might ask the teacher.

One evening later in the week, Ann telephoned, saying, "Something has happened. I don't know what to do." She went on to relate that she had come home from a stressful day at work to find the dishes in the sink and the beds unmade. She had lost her temper and yelled at Mandy before she realized that it was Michael's turn this week to do the dishes and make the beds. "So, what happened then?" I asked. I was confused. Mandy's mother sounded as much elated as she did upset. She replied, "Mandy yelled back at me!" I could hardly believe my ears. It was hard to imagine Mandy standing up to her mother and yelling back. Yet, apparently that was exactly what had happened. Her mother and I were both aware that it was a real breakthrough in Mandy's expressiveness. Ann was concerned, though, that if things were not resolved between them Mandy might retreat back into her shell. After talking it over, she decided to allow a cooling-down period and then apologize to Mandy for yelling before she had her facts straight.

I asked Mandy about the incident the next time I saw her. I asked her how she felt about it. She shrugged and said, "OK," with her shy smile. She seemed to feel no need to pursue the topic. She hadn't yet approached her music teacher and wanted to rehearse it again. She had asked her parents about it. They were in favor of the tutoring and had offered to contact the music teacher for her. "How do you feel about that?" I asked. Mandy shook her head. I said, "This is something you want to do for yourself." She nodded in agreement.

Two weeks later, Mandy's parents asked if they could join us for a few minutes at the beginning of the session. Her mother had a piece of paper in her hand, and for a moment I feared that it was another report card. It turned out to be an application for a summer music camp. Mandy's music teacher had given the class a brochure describing this two-week residential camp in a neighboring state. Her parents were apprehensive about the idea; Mandy had never been away from her family overnight. As we discussed it, Mandy was quietly insistent that she wanted to go. Her parents finally agreed.

I saw Mandy only sporadically in late spring. She had arranged to have after-school tutoring with her music teacher, which was scheduled during our usual appointment time. Summer arrived, and she was gone for two weeks to music camp.

By the time she returned, I had gone on my vacation. When I returned, her family had left town to spend their annual month at Mandy's grandparents' beachfront cottage.

It was early August before I saw Mandy again. She didn't bring her flute. We spent much of our time catching up on how her summer had gone. She had enjoyed music camp and hoped to go again next year. Ann was teaching her to cook and they were spending time together in the kitchen. She was looking forward to school starting in the fall. Very hesitantly, she explained that she would have a busy year with after-school music tutoring. She was also taking piano lessons. When I suggested that maybe she was trying to tell me that she might not have time to come to see me, she replied that her parents thought she should keep coming. I told Mandy that the choice was hers. She didn't have to come back, and she didn't have to stay away. My door would always be open to her if she decided she wanted to talk with me occasionally. She smiled and said she thought she was finished. When her parents came to pick her up, I called them in and we discussed the decision to terminate counseling. They accepted it, although with some reluctance. As they got up to leave, Mandy shyly presented me with a cassette tape, saying that she had recorded a selection she had played for me on her flute.

As they left the office, I realized that Mandy had intended the tape to be her farewell present to me. I inserted it into my tape recorder. The sound of Mandy's flute filled the room. She had recorded Beethoven's "Ode to Joy."

Outcome

Throughout the fall semester, I stayed in touch with Mandy periodically by telephone. School was going well, she said, and everything was "OK" with her family. She was still very involved with her music. When I half-jokingly suggested that she might be a famous flutist some day, she discounted the notion. She didn't want to perform for others. She was looking forward to high school. She was planning to take lots of math and science because she wanted to become a pharmacist.

With Mandy's permission I touched base with Donna Alvarez who reported that she had recently seen Mandy in the school cafeteria sitting at a table with a group of girls. Donna said that, in the brief time she had observed, she had not seen Mandy contribute anything to the conversation but it was obvious to her that Mandy was included. When she saw Mandy in the halls, Mandy was sometimes but not always alone. She had checked on Mandy's progress with her teachers. Two of them told Donna that they occasionally had the students do small-group activities and Mandy had participated in her quiet way.

Discussion

Although I haven't seen Mandy in more than a year, I sometimes reflect on my work with her. Her case reminds me that while diagnosis can illuminate it can also limit our thinking. On the one hand, conceptualizing Mandy's condition as a personality disorder helped me to understand that she may not have been uncomfortable with her isolation even though it concerned those who cared about her. On the other hand, this diagnosis may have led me to expect less of Mandy than she was capable of accomplishing. Did her diagnostic history and my own attempts to categorize her condition lead me to assume she wasn't able to express her feelings directly? Should I have referred her? Might she have become more communicative had she worked with a therapist more skilled in personality disorders?

I also find myself asking, as is often the case with child clients, whose interests were served in counseling? Certainly her parents were pleased with the results. Mandy now behaves more like a "normal" child and is more a part of the family. Her teachers are pleased. She is a bit more integrated with her peers and is a more willing participant in classroom activities. But what of Mandy herself? She didn't request counseling to begin with and was sometimes a reluctant participant in the process. Unlike other clients, I doubt that she will ever articulate to me new self-understandings and positive feelings about herself. Mandy remains a mystery. Were her changes only in her external behavior and only to get others "off her back"? Or does she feel better about herself and her ability to be out in the world?

When I try to imagine Mandy as an adult, I tend to picture her living alone and working as a pharmacist. She is content to deal with prescriptions rather than with people. She continues to enjoy her music and remains in contact with her family. I find it hard to imagine her married with children of her own.

I could be completely wrong. Adolescence, a time of tremendous changes, is just ahead for Mandy. In any event, the answers will come from Mandy herself. If she changed just to please her parents, she will probably revert to her social isolation when she becomes an independent adult. If she likes it out in the world, she will stay there.

Reference

American Psychiatric Association. (2000). *Diagnostic and statistical manual of mental disorders: DSM-IV-TR* (4th ed., text revision). Washington, DC: Author.

Biographical Statement

Barbara Herlihy, PhD, is professor of counselor education at the University of New Orleans. She is a former school counselor and licensed professional counselor in private practice. Barbara has coauthored five books: *The Ethical Standards Casebook*, 4th edition, with Larry Golden; *Ethical, Legal, and Professional Issues in Counseling*, with Theodore P. Remley, Jr.; *Dual Relationships in Counseling; The Ethical Standards Casebook*, 5th edition, and *Boundary Issues in Counseling*, both with Gerald Corey. You can reach Barbara at bxhel@jazz.ucc.uno.edu.

CHAPTER 8

The Boy Who Trashed His Final

Larry B. Golden

Twelve-year-old Joshua is referred because he told his English teacher, "Let my family see me dead!" He is intellectually gifted but very much an underachiever. Josh has a high-performance younger brother, a mother who expects no less from every member of this competitive family, and a father who brings a large dose of ambivalence to most of life's undertakings.

Over time Golden changes his initial DSM-IV-TR diagnosis of Adjustment Disorder with Depressed Mood to Dysthymic Disorder, as it becomes apparent that Josh's problems will not yield to a behavioral approach. Indeed, after an apparent lifting of depression, Josh creates a crisis by throwing his final English exam into the trash can.

Golden uses narrative therapy in response to the crisis. An assumption of the narrative approach is that we create our own reality based on stories we tell ourselves about our experience. This family has created a protective myth around Joshua that is getting in the way of his attempts to individuate. Golden proposes a new, constructive myth.

Finally, this case illustrates that therapeutic gains usually occur day by day, by putting one foot in front of the other; they are not the dramatic outcome of a single intervention, however deft.

J oshua's parents were at the end of their proverbial rope. Joshua was a 12-year-old seventh-grader. He was exhibiting some disturbing behaviors: plucking out his eyebrows and "earning" grades of D's and F's, despite an IQ of 130 and good rapport with his teachers. When he started talking about suicide, his parents decided that he should see a psychologist.

Joshua's father, Raul, was a copywriter at an advertising agency. His mother, Beverly, was an assistant principal at a public elementary school. Joshua's brother, Sidney, though one year younger, was a little taller, handsomer, and a straight-A student. Sid had skipped a year in school, so both brothers were in seventh grade.

Joshua was reputed to be a talented writer. However, regardless of the assigned topic, he turned his stories to themes about magical kingdoms and cataclysmic warfare. Josh's math skills were weak, as compared to his verbal ability. He often failed to turn in work in any of his subjects and was unresponsive to either the carrot or the stick approach.

Joshua was in an English class for gifted and talented (GT) students. Beverly suggested that I call Mrs. Katz, the GT English teacher, who had a close relationship with Josh. Mrs. Katz told me that Josh had a habit of pulling out his eyebrows. He would fall asleep in class. Josh *kvetched* (complained endlessly) about not being liked. Mrs. Katz maintained, however, that while Josh was not popular he was not disliked. He simply didn't respond to other kids and they, in turn, had lost interest in him. She saw him as depressed, withdrawn, and manipulative. She said she had gone the extra mile to help Josh. For example, she would permit him to write about his warfare fantasies instead of insisting that he compose stories on the assigned theme. He was quite willing to talk about personal problems, his "perfect" brother, demanding mother, and angry father. When Josh said, "Let my family see me dead," Mrs. Katz sent him to talk with Mrs. Hernandez, the school counselor.

I called Mrs. Hernandez. Josh had told Mrs. Hernandez of a plan to run away and live in a bat cave near Austin. Josh assured her that the temperature in the cave was a constant 70 degrees Fahrenheit and that the bats, contrary to their grisly reputation, were harmless. Mrs. Hernandez thought Joshua was depressed but not at immediate risk of suicide.

Conceptualization

My primary occupation is that of a college professor. I like to theorize and analyze, which is to say, you are in for a lecture. Also, please enjoy the Yiddishisms. I was raised in a culture that is rich in terminology for human *mishugas* (craziness).

Gifted Underachievers

I have maintained a practice with children and families since 1976. After all these years, I usually get to work with the types of people and problems that interest me. I especially like working with gifted underachievers such as Josh. Most adolescents are poor candidates for psychotherapy. They distrust adults as agents of oppression and regard the therapist as their parents' hired gun. "Off my back" is the teenager's battle cry! Gifted children are more verbal than their peers, and psychotherapy, after all, is a talking cure. They are also fascinated by their own ruminations and mildly curious about psychology as a field of study, a hook into counseling that I'm not above exploiting.

Typically, gifted children are expected to and expect themselves to accomplish great things. When these high standards can't be reached, low self-esteem is the result. Many gifted students, including Josh, though ranking in the top 5 percent or so in intellectual ability, are quite vulnerable to academic failure.

Sibling Rivalry

Another feature of this case was intense sibling rivalry. Parents are often amazed that their naturally born children are so different. It can be no other way. Siblings choose different paths so as to avoid a head-on contest. This is a workable strategy if there is a wide range of competitive arenas. That is, one sibling can invest in music, another in athletics, and so on. In Josh's family, however, academic achievement was everything, and Sidney had cornered the market.

Parents, meaning well, try to convince the losing sibling that he, too, is loved and that they are proud of him as well. However, love and pride are two different things: "You mean you're proud of my crummy grades!" "Well, no, but we're proud of your, well, uhmmm, you play a terrific game of Monopoly!" Such duplicitous reassurance only supports the losing sibling's view of himself as a psychological cripple needy of phony parental bolstering.

Later, we will see that Josh's mother believed that he was expressing contempt for her values when he failed in school. It is more likely that Josh's underachievement could have been a statement, to wit: "This is the only game in town and I lose every time. Why try? Grades are stupid, anyway." Classic sour grapes.

Strategic Family Therapy

It's unusual in my practice to get a request for family therapy. Typically, I get a call from a parent, usually the mother, who is worried about a child's misbehavior. I always ask to see the entire family. Other than in cases when a child must escape a grossly dysfunctional family to survive, it makes sense to include the whole *mishpuchah* (the family at large). Family members live with each other, usually love each other, and are certainly trying to influence each other. So why not invite them to participate together in therapy? I explain that I need everyone's point of view in order to fully understand the child's misbehavior. What's more, if I'm to be effective, I will need everyone's help. Joshua's family, like most, was willing to participate.

Of course, there are different varieties of family therapy. This case is an illustration of strategic family therapy. The strategic therapist tries to change only those aspects of the family system that maintain the symptomatic behavior. Therefore, it falls under the category of brief, rather than depth, psychotherapy. The depth, or psychodynamic, approach assumes that the symptom is merely a cover for underlying pathology. However, this kind of excavation can take years, and this family's insurance coverage provided a strong incentive to complete this work in less than 20 sessions. For the strategic therapist, insight is frosting on the cake and not necessary to resolving the presenting problem.

Narrative Therapy

Strategic family therapists are an eclectic lot. Any technique will do if it brings about the desired change. A technique I like is using stories to help families reframe problems in ways that open up solutions. This method is variously called narrative therapy or story reauthoring.

Families create their own stories and myths. These family myths, like societal ones, serve a purpose. They support family unity, explain the ways of the world, and guide children as they prepare for independence. A myth outlives its usefulness when it too narrowly defines a family member as the sole source of a problem. Such a story encourages blaming and provides little "wiggle room" for therapeutic intervention.

Rational argumentation usually fails to convince a family to give up its outdated mythology because myths are based on irrational beliefs. Instead, the therapist must help the family create a new story to replace the old, a story that serves them better.

Diagnosis

Adjustment Disorder with Depressed Mood (309.0) was my first choice for a *DSM-IV-TR* diagnosis. This is a relatively nonstigmatizing label that assumes that the patient is suffering short-term depression in response to a stressful situation. When the stress is removed or the patient learns to cope, the depression lifts. Later, I changed Josh's diagnosis to Dysthymic Disorder (300.4) because I became convinced that his depression was more or less chronic.

Process

Therapy began on May 4 and continued until October 15 for a total of 20 sessions. Therefore, I met Josh toward the end of one school year and stopped working with him early in the next. Typically, sessions were a three-ring circus, with time reserved for (a) family counseling, (b) individual counseling with Josh, and (c) parent education and counseling. On occasion, the two brothers were seen together.

The First Seven Sessions

Session 1 (5/4). This session was attended by Joshua, his younger brother Sidney, and his parents. Joshua said that he was interested in creative writing and classical music. He admitted that he often failed to turn in assignments. Joshua said that his peers saw him as a "nerd," a "geek," and a "dweeb." Josh was in good health and there was no evidence of alcohol or substance abuse.

Session 2 (5/11). Sid was quick to speak on behalf of his unresponsive older brother. Sid volunteered that Josh's best friend was "Alex the Terminal Weird." Sid, for his part, told me that he enjoyed building model planes, was a fanatic Trekkie (fan of the *Star Trek* television series and movies), loved computers and playing the flute. He added, "I'm the best in seventh grade in algebra! Oh, I know Josh feels terrible when I say that." A Renaissance sib!

Beverly described her family as "a fierce problem-solving outfit" and was optimistic that Josh's problems would be overcome. That was the good news. The bad news was that she saw Josh as a chip off Dad's passive, never-get-ahead block. In fact, though, Raul had a reputation at the advertising agency as being creative and quirky. He was content to leave the management end of the business to the more ambitious types. Sid, on the other hand, was obviously a go-getter like his mother. In a more egalitarian society, Beverly would have been president of General Motors at least. As it was, she was assistant principal of an elementary school.

Sunday was typically "nag and scream" day for Beverly, but this Sunday Raul, at my suggestion, agreed to take charge. Specifically, he would make sure the boys completed their chores. This would not be the first time I would try to shift responsibility for discipline to Raul.

For his part, Josh agreed to an experiment. At least three days during the week, he would complete his assigned work in history no matter how discouraged or bored or lazy or angry he felt.

On May 15, I called Mrs. Katz, Josh's GT English teacher. She reported a "superficial" turnaround. Joshua was completing his assignments, talking to peers, and, as usual, pestering her for personal conferences.

Session 3 (5/18). Beverly was angry. Josh had led her to believe he was giving it his best shot in algebra, and she felt betrayed when he brought home a failing progress report. She demanded a full disclosure. Josh admitted, "I'm failing and I'm not trying." A contrite Josh agreed to complete three chores without even being nagged. Beverly was also angry with Raul. His monitoring of the boys' chores had been half-hearted. They agreed to another therapist injunction: No nagging or punitive measure in regard to the boys could be undertaken prior to both parents consulting with each other. The intent was to encourage Raul to share the disciplinary burden with Beverly. Working together, they could achieve a balance; at odds, they would polarize and undermine each other.

Session 4 (5/25). Josh said that he was trying his best in algebra. He declared that he would try out for the school baseball team next year. I found it hard to picture Josh as a jock.

Session 5 (5/29). A lackluster, low-energy session with Josh. Will he follow through on his promises and thereby, hopefully, pull himself out of depression? I wasn't feeling very optimistic.

On May 31, I received three calls within minutes of each other from Beverly, Mrs. Hernandez (the counselor), and Mrs. Katz. They told the same sorry tale. Josh walked up to Mrs. Katz's desk and dumped his final English exam in the trash can! Later, she retrieved it. Josh had thrown away a C paper that would have earned a passing grade in the course. Instead, he failed GT English for the semester. He also failed history and algebra, though without a dramatic flourish such as ditching a final exam. Beverly wanted Mrs. Katz to count the trashed final. Fortunately, she refused: "I've rescued Josh all year." However, Mrs. Katz deferred to me. If the F would activate Josh's suicidal tendencies, she would reconsider. I didn't think that Josh was suicidal and advised her not to count the trashed exam. Mrs. Hernandez, the school counselor, said that Josh could retake English and algebra during summer school and thereby pass to the next grade. However, if Josh went to summer school, the family would have to cancel plans for a Disney World vacation.

Session 6 (6/5). Gloom and doom. Beverly and Raul were mystified and scared. Why! Why would anyone throw a passing final exam in the trash? Why a preference for failure? How have *we failed?*

I asked each family member to tell me how they would account for the fact that Josh had trashed his final exam.

Josh said, "I don't know." His statement sounded genuine.

Sid shrugged, "He's weird."

Half seriously, Raul said, "Einstein failed seventh-grade math and went on to discover the theory of relativity." But in a more analytical mood, he guessed that Josh had simply given up in his losing rivalry with Sid.

Mom's theory was, "He's shooting the royal bird at our values. He's rejecting everything we believe in and hold dear, the importance of education and trying your best."

I had little use for the family's explanations for Josh's motives. I wanted an explanation that would be empowering, not discouraging. If Sid was correct in his assessment, then there was little hope. Even Freud knew of no cure for being weird.

Raul seemed to think that Josh's intellectual gifts would enable him to go on to great things (such as the theory of relativity) despite a minor setback like failing the seventh grade. However, Josh was no Einstein (it would be fair to assume that Einstein's IQ was somewhat in excess of 130). Dad's concern about Josh's discouragement over Sid's countless achievements deserved serious consideration. I suggested to Sid that if he would fail just one subject, that would certainly be a real shot in the arm for Josh's self-esteem. Sid refused.

Beverly's view, that Josh was rejecting the family values, did not offer a productive lead either. It connected Josh's failures to the vaunted adolescent propensity for rebellion against authority, a tide I had no hope of turning.

No one suggested the role of marital tensions in Josh's behavior, nor did it occur to me at this point in time. Was Joshua subconsciously fighting Raul's battles with Beverly? I would deal with this issue later in therapy.

Any one or all of the above assessments of Josh's motives for trashing his exam could have been correct. On the other hand, since no one knew for certain what the motivation really was, least of all Josh, I decided to invent a motive that would help me do my job.

Session 7 (6/12). Now it was time to plug in my *shpiel* (story) that, God willing, would explain Josh's behavior to everyone's satisfaction. I addressed the family: "Imagine an Olympic athlete. The judge is about to hang the gold medal around his neck, but the athlete steps back and declares, 'I can't accept this award. I've been using steroids to boost my performance.' How would you judge such a person?"

The family consensus was that, while the athlete's use of steroids was reprehensible, declining the gold medal was an honorable and courageous act. I told them that I saw Josh's trashing his final exam as a similar act of conscience. I explained: "Josh uses his reputation as a psychological cripple to get unfair advantage. He *kvetches* to his teachers about how Sid makes him feel stupid, how his mother loves Sid more than him, drops hints about suicide, and plucks his eyebrows. His teachers provide tons of sympathy and demand less of him than the others. When Josh threw his exam in the trash can, he was making a statement, 'Enough is enough. I cannot accept a grade I did not earn!' "

Everyone liked my version. Josh basked in the glory of his gutsy choice. Now Josh's parents could shift their guilt for Josh's failures to his very recently broadened shoulders.

Of course, Mom stopped trying to get the teacher to credit him for the trashed exam. I pointed out that Josh would no longer tolerate such rescuing.

Josh was left with no reasonable alternative other than to pick up the burden of manly responsibility I had fashioned for him. He agreed not to solicit therapy from his teachers; one therapist was enough for anyone. Mrs. Katz was relieved to hear that she was out of the psychotherapy business and could resume her chosen occupation as a teacher.

As for Sid, he was advised to *shlep nachus* (bring home honors that would reflect well on his parents) as he'd always done, assured by me that Josh had the strength to bear up under his younger brother's success.

The Remaining Thirteen Sessions

I wish I could say that my clever story about the Olympics resolved Josh's problems of underachievement, low self-esteem, and depression. In fact, my reframe gave the family a different perspective, one that enhanced everyone's self-esteem. However, the school year was over, and Josh would have to await the start of summer school to demonstrate any renewed commitment to academics. Much work remained. Which is to say, like most of us, Josh took one step backward (at least!) for every two forward.

There were several obstructions besides Josh's brute inertia. I knew that I would have to do something to defuse the sibling rivalry. As things were, Josh would rather fail than risk a head-on contest with Sid. Further, long-standing marital problems had surfaced.

<u>Defusing Sibling Rivalry.</u> In an individual session, Josh told me that he thought his parents loved Sid more than him because Sid was an academic superstar. I pointed out that Josh was mistaking gratitude for love. When Sid looked good, Beverly and Raul looked good. Sid brought home the bacon, and his parents were appreciative.

"So what do you want from them, Josh?" I asked. "Love? Would you believe them if they told you that they loved you as much as Sid?"

"Not really," said Josh.

I told Josh that I thought that his parents already loved him enough, maybe too much.

Josh decided that love was hard to define. Instead, he would attempt to win his parents' respect. I told Josh that I didn't think he would have to match Sid's stellar performance to do this. But he would have to become a *mensch*, a man of his word, a person others could depend on.

Josh was eager to tell his parents of his quest for their respect. I advised against a premature spilling of the beans: "Go for it! Maybe they'll notice."

I wanted to make the competitive nature of this family explicit and thereby less destructive. In a conjoint session, I asked the family members to line up on a winner-to-loser continuum. Sid was numero uno, then Bev, then Raul, with "the dweeb" bringing up the rear. Then I asked the parents to objectively evaluate and compare each brother's abilities as if they were judges at a county livestock fair. Raul and Beverly didn't care for this crude exercise. It focused unpleasantly on the way that both boys (indeed, even the parents) were expected to be shown as the family's prize cows! It was also true that these parents loved their children. But the distinction between unconditional love and pride in a child's achievements had become blurred. In relation to Beverly, Sid saw himself as a *nachus* machine, Josh as a source of bitter *tzuris*. (*Nachus* is the joy children bring to their parents through their positive achievements, while *tzuris* is the heartache children cause their parents by misbehaving.)

In a session that included only the boys, I asked for a disclosure of slings and arrows, verbal and physical, that each brother employed against the other. I wanted to get these weapons out on the table where they could be dealt with. Sid told of Josh's constant physical attacks over the years. These had stopped in recent months. I'd love to attribute the cessation of violence to counseling, but I suspect it had much more to do with the fact that Sid was now as big as Josh. In the realm of verbal weaponry, Josh's best shot was to call Sid "mama's boy" or "fag," while Sid would retaliate with "loser" or "psycho." They agreed not to use these epithets against each other for one week. So as not to leave them naked and unarmed, I gave each brother a secret and terrible name to use in case of dire need. Josh was instructed to lambaste Sid with *schlemiel* and Sid was to smear Josh with *schlamazel*. (Both are Yiddish words that mean "jerk," more or less.) The intervention had the desired effect; it took the sting out of the verbal cuts.

Encouraging Joshua to Accept Responsibility. Josh told me of a dream in which he forgot his books and registration card on the very first day of summer school. You don't have to be Carl Jung to interpret this one: Josh was worried that he would mess up his big chance to prove himself. Beverly and Raul were also anxious about summer school. I was, too. In Josh's presence, I asked Beverly and Raul if they wanted to assume responsibility for Josh's passing summer school. They declined. I asked them if they held me responsible, God forbid. They let me off the hook as well. So who would be entitled to the credit or blame for passing or failing? The man himself!

As summer school got under way, I assigned Josh the task of keeping a daily log of his progress in both of his summer school classes, English and algebra, and issuing brief weekly reports to his parents. Grades aside, these (hopefully) truthful, dependable reports would accrue to Josh's status as a *mensch*.

In his first official report Josh predicted an A in English and a B in algebra. By the fourth week, however, Josh had downgraded his estimate to an A and a D. His final grades after the six-week summer term were an A and an F. *Oy gevalt!*

Josh was promoted on the condition that he repeat and pass algebra during the fall term.

Nail biting had taken the place of eyebrow plucking when Josh was in his anxiety mode. But he wanted to stop being anxious, not merely substitute one symptom for another. He asked my advice. I told him that maybe a little anxiety wasn't so bad. He decided to substitute clicks with his ball-point pen for nail biting.

I helped Josh compose "awful angry notes" to send to Beverly when she got on his case. How did Woody Allen put it? "I don't get angry, I just grow a tumor." For Josh, substitute an F for the tumor! Beverly said that she would much prefer Josh's nasty notes to his being passive-aggressive.

Marital Issues. I scheduled a parents-only session in preparation for the new school year. I urged that the home-school team go into action at the first indication of serious goofing off and vigorously pursue evidence of same. Raul was worried that Josh would feel that he wasn't trusted. Trust, shmust! Parents should understand that their teens are in the business of outfoxing them. Raul agreed to do the detective work and check on Josh's schoolwork, but his heart wasn't in it.

I knew that trust was also an issue between Beverly and Raul. Raul felt bossed around by Beverly. He handled this in a passive-aggressive manner by not following through. Consequently, Beverly saw him as unreliable and untrustworthy.

Although Beverly and Raul had not contracted for marital counseling, I observed that their issues were getting in the way of Josh's progress. I pointed out certain parallels between Beverly's feelings towards Raul and Josh and their reactions to her.

Raul complained that he had sold out his dream of being a novelist to earn a living as a hack at an ad agency. He wanted to blame Beverly for this disappointment. Beverly, however, was angry, even despairing, about Raul's lack of ambition. He had languished as an advertising writer while others had risen to managerial positions and partnerships. Beverly saw the same self-defeating tendencies in Joshua. She was astonished that Raul still had a yen to be a novelist since he hadn't written anything but advertising copy since he was in college.

"That's the point," said Raul.

"So whose fault is it?" asked Beverly.

"I wonder if Joshua will ever take a risk," said I.

Raul corrected me, "Raul, not Joshua."

My slip wasn't lost on either partner. Raul and Josh, the two *schlemiels*. I asked Raul if he would tolerate one of my lectures. He said that he would. My message to Raul was that he could set a good example for his sons and win his wife's respect by being a *mensch*. Either get to work on a novel or give it up, but stop blaming Beverly or the advertising agency. What's more, I told him to stand up to Beverly and stop being passive-aggressive in their relationship.

I asked Beverly if she could imagine feeling good about Josh settling for B's or Raul not advancing his advertising career. She replied that B's would be OK but not wonderful and the same went for Raul. Josh was smart enough to get A's, and Raul was capable of advancing himself. Still, she had been in the education business long enough to know that there are different kinds of smarts. Josh's and Raul's dreamy world view and their ambivalence toward academic and career achievement would not yield A's or promotions no matter how hard they were pushed. Were Josh and Raul quirky guys who didn't fit the common mold? Or were they bent on resisting Beverly's push for excellence even at the expense of their own advancement? Although there may have been some truth in both scenarios, I suggested that she buy into the quirky guys idea for the sake of peace and quiet in the family.

This session was as far as either parent wanted to go with marital counseling.

Outcome

Josh predicted a good first six-weeks report card. The parents promised a celebration of large proportions if Josh's prophecy came true. So what do you think happened?

Good news! Mostly B's, no D's or F's. I praised Josh to the sky for delivering on his word, a more significant indicator of maturity than mere good grades.

Usually I don't hear from clients after termination. In this case, Beverly kept me posted with occasional notes for about six months. The gist was that Josh was doing well, Sid was doing great, and she and Raul had found some peace of mind. Here are two of the notes.

Note (12/9)

We survived the second six weeks. Josh slipped a bit, 95 down to 78 in French and 80 to 70 in algebra. He knows we are disappointed, and for what it may be worth, I think he's putting out a bit more effort. I guess you could say that we are trying to ride the tide. Sid turned out another superb performance. Six A's! I've enclosed one of our family photos; the boys mentioned that you might like one. Please know we will feel free to call you at the first sign of a real crisis; we'll handle the small everyday ones!

Note (1/21)

Things running fairly smoothly. Josh brought home a progress report for algebra 89 average! Long may it continue. He wants to go to France this summer in an exchange program so he knows he must keep his grades up. We let him set the parameters, and he suggested an 83 minimum in everything. Now we wait and see. Sid was the school team alternate to the Math Counts competition at the University of Texas, and he placed fifth among all alternates who competed. Hubby and I are continuing to enjoy the challenges of adolescence. We're still able to smile, a positive sign.

My sense of these two notes was that the bitter, baffled reaction to Josh's miserable school performance had abated. There was a rueful acceptance of the *tzuris* that parenting holds in store. And, of course, Josh was passing his subjects, working up to *his* expectations and current capabilities.

Discussion

My initial attempt at getting rid of Josh's negative behaviors resulted in superficial changes and set the stage for a dramatic crisis, trashing the final exam. The reframing of Josh's self-defeating behavior as an Olympic myth had positive results. Josh had been saddled with a myth that he was a psychological cripple, needy of external support. I meant it when I had told Josh that his parents loved him too much. Their well-meaning attempts to bolster his self-esteem only demonstrated that he was needy of special help. The trashing of the exam could easily have been the "nail in the coffin," confirming this family's worst fears about Joshua and themselves. The Olympic myth portrayed Josh as being irrevocably committed to a course of autonomy, no longer willing to accept undeserved advantage.

One myth that therapists are stuck with is that one brilliant therapeutic stroke can reverse years of complex behavior patterning. This particular myth is canonized at professional conferences where one witnesses dramatic "cures" by the great gurus of psychotherapy. True cures? For my part, therapy is a little bit of this, a little bit of that, and then maybe a partial solution.

This family was in many respects a mirror of my own family of origin. I, like Josh, had a hard time making a comeback from a one-down sibling rivalry. It's important to know that Sid (and my brother) also paid a heavy price, for Sid was never sure if he was valued for anything other than his achievements. Working with a client and a family that is similar to your own is tricky business. To the extent that therapists are aware of their own family dynamics, they bring the benefits of personal experience and insight to their work. On the other hand, ignorance can lead to problems with countertransference and projection. For this reason I believe that counselors should get therapy for themselves intermittently throughout their professional lifetimes.

Reference

American Psychiatric Association. (2000). *Diagnostic and statistical manual of mental disorders: DSM-IV-TR* (4th ed., text revision). Washington, DC: Author.

Biographical Statement

Larry B. Golden, PhD, is associate professor and coordinator of the counseling program at the University of Texas at San Antonio. He is a licensed psychologist and has maintained a part-time private practice since 1976. He specializes in counseling with children and families. Larry has published several books, including *Psychotherapeutic Techniques in School Psychology, Helping Families Help Children: Family Interventions with School-Related Problems, Preventing Adolescent Suicide, The Ethical Standards Casebook,* 4th edition, and *Case Studies in Marriage and Family Therapy.* You can reach Larry at lgolden@utsa.edu.

CHAPTER 9

Will He Choose Life?

J. Jeffries McWhirter

This case study consists of a single interview. It is a detailed account of an assessment of suicide potential. As McWhirter probes for crucial information, we are privy to the process by which the clinician arrives at a conclusion as to whether or not 12-year-old Mark is at risk of suicide.

McWhirter explores such factors as family history, depression, and religious beliefs as they correlate with suicide risk. Client confidentiality is discussed as a related issue.

I have published a number of articles and book chapters on the topic of youth depression and suicide prevention that have had a curious impact on my small private practice. I find myself at times, more often than I might wish, called upon to assess suicide potential. Of course, this kind of responsibility weighs heavily. I listen carefully to a teacher or parent or young person as I try to answer an important question: What is the probability that this particular youngster will choose death over life?

Most mental health professionals will be confronted with this question at one time or another. I assume that they confront, as I do, their own underlying fears: Will I be sufficiently perceptive to discern whether the youngster is a potential suicide? Can I provide alternatives to prevent a suicide attempt? What can I tell the parents to help them help this youngster? It occurs to me that providing a step-by-step review of an actual suicide assessment interview might be helpful to other mental health professionals. My format here provides excerpts from an interview and my accompanying comments as I try to determine suicide potential in a client.

Conceptualization

This case is based on an initial assessment interview that I conducted with Mark Thomas, a 12-year-old middle school student, and his mother, Sally. Sally contacted me regarding Mark's thoughts about suicide after a consultation with Mark's school counselor. Prior to the following interview, I had a telephone conversation with Sally regarding Mark's suicide thoughts, his previous therapy experiences, and their current family situation. I learned that Mark lived with his divorced mother and a younger sister. He had frequent and consistent contact with his father, who lived with his second wife a short distance from Mark's home.

I had also received a call from Mark's school counselor, Paula, whom I had known and worked with for 15 years. Paula's estimation was that an evaluation was definitely called for. She said that Mark had low self-esteem and was having peer adjustment problems, and that there had been previous suicide experiences in the family. Apparently, Mark's mother had made a suicide attempt, and her sister (Mark's aunt) had killed herself some years earlier. Because Paula is not an alarmist, I took her assessment seriously and made an effort to schedule an appointment with Mark as soon as possible after I received his mother's phone call.

In a suicide assessment interview the therapist needs to establish rapport and a therapeutic alliance very quickly. I believe that showing empathy, warmth, and genuineness and practicing good communication skills (as described by Carl Rogers) are essential in an assessment interview and in the beginning stages of therapy. Having established rapport, the therapist can proceed to specific assessment questions to determine suicide potential.

Process

Mark arrived at my office accompanied by his mother. He was neatly and appropriately dressed and was cooperative throughout the interview. He displayed adequate interpersonal skills but subdued affect. He presented himself in a serious fashion and was open about his personal life.

Mark told me that he had strong academic skills. He saw himself as intelligent, based on the fact that he was enrolled in several honors classes. Mark described himself as an accomplished instrumental musician. He was worried about his lack of athletic ability and his image with peers. Mark told me that he was called a "nerd" because his peers thought that he studied all the time. In fact, he expressed an aversion to his teachers and classes. Problems with his mother also surfaced.

Counselor:	So why did your mom want you to see me?
Mark:	Because we've had a lot of communication difficulties. I guess she feels that I don't talk to her enough, but she just asks me to do things. It's always, "Here, Mark, do this. Mark, do that."
Counselor:	Is she right about you not talking to her enough?
Mark:	Not particularly. Whenever she wants to know anything, I tell her. Mostly stuff that I think is personal I keep to myself. Most of the time she blames me for things.

Counselor:	Could you give me an example?
Mark:	Yeah. I think it sort of is my fault though. One weekend I was going on a camping trip and she never asked if I needed to go buy stuff I needed for the camping trip. I didn't tell her because I forgot. But, if she would have asked me, I would have remembered. So my scout leader called me and I asked my mom, and she goes, "Why didn't you tell me about this before? Now I've scheduled some things."

Comment. Some of Mark's conflicts have begun to surface. He implied that his mother was to blame for their poor communication and then immediately shifted the blame to himself, perhaps indicating low self-esteem and self-punitive thoughts. Adolescent suicide attempters display less positive self-esteem than nonattempters, and their negative thoughts and attributions are an important part of their problem.

Counselor:	Things aren't going well with your friends. You mentioned being criticized. . . .
Mark:	No, those are not friends but stoners that criticize. Ninety-five percent of school is made up of stoners and the rest are jocks.
Counselor:	Are you a jock or a stoner?
Mark:	Neither, I'm a nerd.

Comment. In Mark's school, "stoners" were youngsters who were perceived to use drugs and alcohol. Drug and alcohol use are prevalent among suicidal adolescents. Although I did not inquire directly, Mark's response suggested that he was not using drugs. On the other hand, he appeared not to have a very extensive peer network and felt alienated. Mark described an incident that supported this view in which two younger friends agreed to meet him but left him stranded. Loneliness and lack of social support are correlated with suicide attempts.

Counselor:	Do you get down in the dumps?
Mark:	No. I get depressed when I can't figure out something or do something.
Counselor:	Like what? Math, you mean?
Mark:	Yeah, math, science, stuff like that. And when I get tons of homework piled up on me and it's all due the next day.
Counselor:	You seem overwhelmed. But you're not down in the dumps?
Mark:	No. There's no reason to be.

Comment. I was frankly surprised at Mark's answer about depression. Most youngsters will admit to depression and to thinking about suicide when asked. Had I pressed too deeply or too quickly? Was Mark unaware of being depressed, or was he aware but unwilling to admit it to me? Or was Mark really not depressed? Keep in mind that the relationship between depression and suicide during adolescence is not straightforward. Suicidal behavior may result from depression, but a child need not be depressed for suicide to occur. And, of course, depression does not always lead to suicide. Depression remains, however, the most common denominator among both suicide attempters and completers.

Mark portrayed his father as being permissive but short-tempered. He described his big-brother role with his younger sister. Their relationship alternated between teasing and fighting and Mark's acting like her parent. This led to Mark's discussion of feelings about himself.

Mark:	I have sort of low self-esteem. I mean you got to feel good about yourself.
Counselor:	What do you mean?
Mark:	I don't feel good about myself. But I feel that God put me on earth for some reason, for something special.

Comment. A belief in God and the possibility of an afterlife tends to motivate against suicide. I was pleased that Mark coupled his belief with the view that he was put on earth for a reason. Lack of purpose in life is correlated with suicide attempts and compilations.

Counselor:	You have some purpose being here on earth.
Mark:	Some purpose, yeah.
Counselor:	But you haven't figured it out yet?
Mark:	No. I'm waiting for that day to come.
Counselor:	Does it seem hopeless?
Mark:	Yeah.

Comment. A feeling of hopelessness is characteristic of suicidal children. Of course, *hopeless* was my word, not his. It seemed time for a direct assault on the possible intention of suicide.

Counselor:	You've talked about low self-esteem, and you've talked about being lonely, and about not being able to figure out your purpose in life.
Mark:	Yeah.
Counselor:	And even though you say you are not depressed, it sounds like school's not going well and home's not going very well. Maybe this will sound funny coming out of the blue, but have you thought about doing anything to hurt yourself?
Mark:	Yeah. Lots of times.
Counselor:	Tell me about it.
Mark:	I thought I'd kill myself once.
Counselor:	When was that?
Mark:	A couple of years ago and again maybe three months ago. I didn't like the way band was going. My teacher was always critical. And really, it wasn't my fault. I got so many detention passes because other people wouldn't leave me alone.
Counselor:	So you were getting in trouble.

Mark: Yeah. I wanted to drown myself in my pool. But I figured I
                   shouldn't do it. That action would hurt my mom. So I didn't
                   do it.

Comment. A central question for the suicide candidate is, "How will you do
it?" The vagueness or specificity of his or her plan helps determine the extent of
the risk. By asking this question one can also determine the reversibility of the
action and the seriousness of the client's intent. Mark's plan of drowning in his
swimming pool was relatively low risk compared to using a gun. His concerns
about his mother's feelings also boded well.

I wanted to know if he had considered the range of suicidal possibilities
open to him. Second, I wanted to know how often Mark had had suicidal thoughts
and whether these thoughts were a recent phenomenon. Had he been
contemplating suicide for a long time? Third, I wanted to see if there was a link
between the specific suicide ideation and other events in his life.

Counselor: Why the swimming pool? Why drown?
Mark: Because the swimming pool is a way out. I mean I couldn't
                   stab myself. I can't stand the sight of blood . . . or pain.
Counselor: Have you thought about other ways?
Mark: I thought of strangling myself one day, but there was no
                   place to do it. I thought about many ways to kill myself, but
                   then I thought, "No, there's no reason to."
Counselor: When was this?
Mark: Oh, about two or three months ago. Then I started doing
                   better and I stopped thinking about it.
Counselor: Two or three months ago it sounds like you were going
                   through hell.
Mark: Yeah.
Counselor: Had you thought about killing yourself even before that?
Mark: No, except that time two years ago.
Counselor: How would you have drowned yourself?
Mark: Oh, just in the bathtub.
Counselor: Any other ideas?
Mark: Yeah. I thought of diving off a bridge onto the freeway. But I
                   figured I'd just end up in the hospital.

Comment. It became clear to me that Mark had not developed a specific
plan. Drowning oneself in a bathtub or swimming pool, while possible, is unlikely.
More lethal methods had been rejected. His concern about the pain of the act and
about botching it and ending up in the hospital weighed against a suicide attempt.

Counselor: If you were to take your own life, what would come after,
                   would there be anything for you after that?
Mark: I don't know.
Counselor: I don't think any of us know, but what do you think?

Mark:	I would probably get stuck in the middle as a ghost, trying to redeem my life so I'd get through it. I'd have to work out bad stuff, like stealing. I stole something, but I had to return it.
Counselor:	No kidding?
Mark:	Yeah.
Counselor:	You mean you *had* to take it back?
Mark:	I didn't get caught. I felt so bad, I had to return it. I returned it, and I said "Thank you very much, here it is." I felt relieved.
Counselor:	So you believe that even if you were to kill yourself, you would still have to come back and make up for things that you did wrong?
Mark:	Yeah.

Comment. Mark had a well-developed superego and a belief that suicide would not be an end to his responsibilities to make things right. I wanted to reinforce this attitude. A strong sense of responsibility to family and friends motivates against suicide.

Counselor:	What about right now?
Mark:	I'm doing better. My schoolwork is shaping up. I got a couple more friends. I do more things.
Counselor:	What would have helped you when things were really bad?
Mark:	Maybe people listening to me. I need to say my problems. I didn't want to talk to my mom because she gets too emotional.
Counselor:	Well, that's what counselors are for! I'll be here if you want to talk. But there's something I want from you right now. I want an agreement, a contract that you will not do anything to hurt yourself during the time that you and I are talking to each other.
Mark:	OK.
Counselor:	I'll give you a phone number, and if you need to talk, you give me a call. I want you to agree to talk to me before you do anything to hurt yourself.
Mark:	OK.

Comment. The formal signing of a contract makes the commitment more concrete. The contract buys time for the client to consider solutions and to learn new skills.

After I met with Mark, I interviewed Mark's mother, Sally. I wanted her impressions of Mark's suicide potential, and I wanted to know more about the family's suicide history. I also wanted to discuss a therapeutic contract.

| Counselor: | How are things with Mark from your perspective? |
| Sally: | Well, I had thought that they were going pretty well. He's basically a good kid. Does well in school. Mark has always |

	been reticent, reluctant to try anything. Cautious to the extreme.
Counselor:	Not impulsive?
Sally:	Right.

Comment. Impulsivity is a major concern when assessing suicide potential. Mark's obsessive need to think things over would function as a safety check.

Counselor:	Would he have known of anyone who has committed suicide?
Sally:	Not that I know of. My sister did about 10 years ago. And she was 25. She was always a bit bothered. Sue had a gun and ammunition because she had intended to kill her husband and herself. It was a strange death. She was left-handed and was shot right-handed, and so I have never accepted the fact that she killed herself. But I have accepted the fact that her intentions were there. So it was either a scuffle or something went on, or whatever. And I did not tell the children because I thought Mark's father might use that against me. And about five years ago I tried to kill myself. I was depressed over where I was, financially strapped. I ran my car in the garage for a quarter of a tank of gas.
Counselor:	But you didn't die.
Sally:	It was a dumb thing, in my garage. I wasted $5 of gas before I realized what I was doing. I turned the car off and then broke down. It was kind of like, you know, it was a weird thing. Being alone and being in such despair . . . and me driving home and thinking, "I don't care anymore, I don't care who I hurt, I don't care who it touches, I've just had all I can take, I can't deal with another thing." So I know when someone is to that point of desperation that they can't be talked out of it. You almost have to be held down until it passes.
Counselor:	Would Mark have known about your attempt?
Sally:	No. A couple of friends knew.
Counselor:	And you're surmising that he doesn't know about his aunt?
Sally:	He asked me what happened, and I said it was an accident because I felt that that was not a lie, but I didn't need to tell him all of the facts. Quite frankly, because I didn't feel like I knew them all. And I couldn't be objective about Susie's death, and so when they asked about it, they asked if it was a car accident, and I said it was an accident. I have never lied to them, but I have not given the whole picture.

Comment. In this family suicide was seen as a solution to problems. Unfortunately, suicide tends to run in families. I hoped that Mark was unaware of the actual incidents.

Sally:	What are your impressions? Am I in a crisis situation with this child?
Counselor:	I don't think so. I've asked him to sign a contract with me that he not do anything, but I don't think that you're in a crisis situation right now. He's going to need to attend to feelings of loneliness, feeling like he's not really fitting in at school. These are important self-esteem issues, and I do think that counseling can help. I would suggest that I see Mark for 10 sessions. In time, I'll know more about Mark's suicide potential.
Sally:	All right. But he does lie. I do warn you about that. He's done that with me a couple of times and it's real hard to catch, but then he has come to me almost immediately, "I told you something that is not true." So, my perception is that he is basically honest but he will lie.
Counselor:	I would suggest another appointment in three days.

Comment. Ordinarily I do not see clients so soon. Even though I did not think Mark was at immediate risk, I was worried about Sally's comment about lying. Better to be safe than sorry. I was convinced that if Mark could talk through his stresses and conflicts, alternatives would emerge. An important factor in suicide is the individual's dichotomous thinking patterns that tend to limit alternatives. I wanted to teach Mark to expand his black-or-white perspective to shades of gray.

Mark returned to the room. He signed a contract that stated that he would not do anything to hurt himself during the time we worked together. I asked him to call me should he feel especially depressed.

Outcome

I worked with Mark on a weekly basis. After three months we moved to twice-per-month meetings. Mark reported that he was feeling better and that his conflict with his mother had become less intense. He said that there had been no recurrence of suicidal thoughts. Sally said that she saw improvement in Mark; he smiled more and his attitude was more positive.

Discussion

I concluded that Mark was not actively suicidal. Therefore, I got a written contract from Mark stating that he would not attempt suicide, and I set up an appointment to begin therapy with the goal of reducing depression. But what if I had assessed Mark's situation as acute? What steps should be taken if a child is evaluated as actively suicidal? In that case, the child must be supervised constantly until the crisis passes, usually about 24 to 72 hours. Help the child and the family find ways to lessen the pain. If communication can be opened and stress can be eased, the immediate and overwhelming sense of hopelessness will diminish. Finally, both medication and hospitalization are possible courses of action.

Confidentiality with youngsters this age is a difficult issue. Parents want and need to know some information, even though the right of confidentiality resides with the client. The basic rule that I follow and which I explained to Mark is that I try to do what is in the client's best interest. I honor confidentiality unless I think the client is in clear danger.

Biographical Statement

J. Jeffries McWhirter, PhD, is professor of counseling psychology at Arizona State University and maintains a private practice in psychology. He is designated as a diplomate in counseling psychology by the American Board of Professional Psychology. He was a senior Fulbright-Hays fellow (1977–78) at Hacettepe University, Ankara, Turkey, and a senior Fulbright scholar at Catholic College of Education in Sydney, Australia (1984–85). Dr. McWhirter has published widely on the topic of at-risk youth, adolescent depression, and suicide. His latest book, written with his adult children, is *At-Risk Youth: A Comprehensive Response,* published by Brooks/Cole in 1998. You can reach Jeff at mcwhirter@asu.edu.

CHAPTER 10

The Girl with Painful Steps

Barbara Peeks Dunn and Ray L. Levy

This case presents an 11-year-old girl who walks on crutches because her right leg is swollen and sore to the touch. The cause of her affliction (Conversion Disorder, *DSM-IV-TR*) is unknown and doctors are baffled. As a last resort, the orthopedic surgeon refers Jenny to Ray Levy, then a psychology student intern at Children's Hospital, Virginia Commonwealth University, in Richmond. The physician's poor opinion of psychology is no secret, and figuring out how to cure Jenny and simultaneously impress the doctor gives Levy quite a headache.

Levy is committed to a family therapy model but hampered by the fact that the parents are separated and living on different coasts. The father, who is visiting, is due to return to his home in two days. His imminent departure makes Jenny's symptoms and Levy's much worse.

A call to Barbara Peeks Dunn leads to her serving as Levy's supervisor in the case. Levy consulted weekly with Peeks Dunn by telephone. The method of treatment is strategic family therapy, in which the child's social situation is reorganized to eliminate the cause of her symptoms. Peeks Dunn chooses a behavioral metaphor for the precipitating event, and she formulates

A brief account of this case appeared in "Strategies for Solving Children's Problems Understood as Behavioral Metaphors" by Barbara Peeks, 1989, *Journal of Strategic and Systemic Therapies, 8*(1), p. 22. Adapted by permission.

directives for Levy to give the family (he writes them down on 3-by-5-inch cards to ensure accuracy and puts them in his pocket). Rather than attempt to change Jenny, Peeks Dunn, and Levy design a plan to change the conditions, interactions, and relationships in her environment. We leave it to you, and the orthopedic surgeon, to evaluate the results.

The Therapist's View

The head of the orthopedic surgery department at Children's Hospital approached me in the hallway: "I have a case for you or one of your types." He was known to look down on psychology as a profession, and he would refer a patient only as a last resort. Eleven-year-old Jenny, he continued, had experienced leg problems for one year. The cause was unknown and, in fact, her symptoms had baffled her doctors for some time. Finally, she had been admitted to a children's hospital the previous week to undergo diagnostic tests in addition to the physical therapy she had been receiving for several weeks. Still, her doctors could find no basis for her problem. Thus, as a last resort, she was referred to the psychology department, where I was serving as a student intern.

The doctor described the symptoms Jenny was experiencing. She walked on crutches because her right leg from the midcalf down was swollen and sore to the touch. Her left leg had similar symptoms but less severe. She had limited flexion and mobility and was in extreme pain, yet a diagnosis proved difficult. Sympathetic reflex dystrophy was ruled out because of the bilaterality of her symptoms. In addition to five weeks of physical therapy, myriad tests and physical treatments had been tried to determine the cause of and to relieve the pain, including casting her leg. Jenny's pain would temporarily abate but not disappear.

Her disorder clearly was hindering and negatively affecting her life. She had been a cheerleader but due to her symptoms had dropped out of the squad. Moreover, her social life became more limited due to her lack of mobility. On further investigation of the situation, I found that Jenny's parents were separated. Her father was living on the West Coast; her mother and the children were residing on the East Coast. Her father came to visit every six to eight weeks; he was visiting at the present time but was leaving in two days. When I talked to Jenny alone, she was very open and sociable with me until I inquired about how things were at home. When I asked her about her parents' separation and her feelings about her father, she began to cry and stated that she wanted to go back to her room. She got up on her crutches and hurried out of my office. I followed her to her ward, where she found her father and collapsed in his arms crying.

Her father later came to my office and in a sad manner told me about his estranged wife. He said he still loved her, but she insisted on running around with other men. He told me that his wife's father had become ill a year ago. At about the same time he had become so severely depressed about their marital problems that he decided to send his wife and children to the opposite coast to live with her parents. He sincerely related how concerned he and his wife were about Jenny and said they would be willing to be a part of her rehabilitation.

That night I went home with a terrific headache as I tried to figure out how I was going to simultaneously impress the doctor and cure Jenny in two days. Jenny's symptoms were clearly related to her father's imminent departure since her symptoms had recently exacerbated, which they always did when he was about to leave.

I wondered if I could relieve Jenny's pain using hypnosis. While I might have been able to alleviate some of the pain in this way, I knew that unless I did something to affect her environment (i.e., her parents), the relief would be only temporary. I had recently begun reading *Leaving Home* by Jay Haley (1980) and *Strategic Family Therapy* by Cloe Madanes (1981) and had attended a workshop in Washington, D.C., presented by the authors. It was there that I met Barbara Peeks, who had been trained by them. We went to lunch, she told me about some of her cases, she advised me on one of my cases, and she gave me her card. Wanting to give strategic family therapy a serious try, I decided to contact Barbara in Nebraska to see if she would serve as my supervisor by phone.

The Supervisor's View

"Ray Levy? Who is Ray Levy?" I asked myself. "Oh, yes, we met in Washington, D.C. We had lunch together." "Would you be willing to help me?" he asked. "I'll be glad to help," I replied, happy to know that I had sparked an interest in family therapy in a young therapist. He was anxious to do a good job and concerned that this would be the last opportunity Jenny's parents might have for conjoint therapy. Ray was in a doctoral program that was teaching psychodynamic approaches to problem situations, which he did not feel suited the particular characteristics of this case. He lacked training in family therapy techniques and was asking me for supervision.

According to my notes of Ray's first telephone call, he presented the following facts about Jenny and her family. Her pain was from her lower calf to her foot, and it was moving up her leg. The symptom began soon after her mother and siblings had left her father to move to the grandparents' town. Jenny was a middle child of five (ages 14, 13, 11, 6, and 5). The father was living on the opposite coast and was now visiting; he was 34, a bricklayer, and called himself "pathetic." The parents have been married 14 years. The father said that his wife runs around and is a pathological liar. Both parents drink. The father was so depressed a year ago that he sent his wife and children to his wife's parents. The maternal grandfather recently died.

The most startling aspect of the situation that Ray described was the fact that one of the doctors involved with Jenny had described Jenny's worst scenario as amputation of the leg. Here was a child who might lose a leg, and I had just accepted responsibility for phone supervision of a therapist I did not know! I was uncertain of Ray's abilities, knowledge of family systems, his willingness to be directive, or even if the information he had presented to me was correct. But I did know that he was willing to try new approaches, as evidenced by the fact that he had used my interventions with his other case. Knowing the doctor's lack of respect for psychological intervention, I felt he would not attempt another referral for Jenny to the psychology department if Ray was unsuccessful with the case. The medical community had almost given up on Jenny, and I felt sympathy for her situation and respect for the young therapist who was willing to tackle such a difficult case. I would try my best to help Ray. I solicited his pledge to follow my directions as closely as possible, even if he did not understand strategic family therapy in all its details.

Conceptualization

The Supervisor's View

Strategic family therapy is a directive therapy that seeks to reorganize the child's social situation to eliminate the cause of the child's symptom(s). A directive is developed based on the type and severity of the problem and the goal of therapy. The type of directive that is chosen is also influenced by the therapist's understanding of the behavioral metaphor. The directive should ideally eliminate the presenting problem and also alleviate or change the problem in the larger social situation, which is hypothesized to be the source of the child's problem.

Parents who seek a mental health professional for therapy trust and expect the professional to be expert in the area of solving children's problems. They come to therapy seeking advice, direction, and solutions for problems they themselves have not been able to solve. Parents will readily follow a therapist's advice and direction if the therapist takes proper care to involve them in establishing a plausible definition of the problem and reasonable treatment goals.

It was essential for me to be certain that Ray understood the importance of each directive and why he was asking the family to take each action. Without presenting him with a semester-long course in family therapy, I emphasized the following ideas:

1. He must focus the entire session on what everyone in the family could do to help Jenny. In other words, he had to ensure that every action he recommended was designed to eliminate Jenny's symptoms, not to provide insight or allow the family members to express feelings.

2. He must believe that Jenny's symptoms were benevolent and protective and that subconsciously she was attempting to help solve some larger problem that was causing distress for her family.

3. He must be in control of the session, must believe in the effectiveness of the directives he proposed, and must convince the family members to take action to help Jenny.

Before a strategy can be developed to solve a problem situation, a hypothesis for the cause of the problem must first be formulated. It is helpful to think about (a) problems evident in a child's social situation and (b) behavioral metaphors.

Ray's initial outline of Jenny's problems included (a) her father's depression and low self-esteem, (b) family transitions (i.e., a move and the grandfather's death), (c) the parent's marriage and separation, (d) the parents' drinking, and (e) her mother's lying and infidelity. One of these problems, a combination of these problems, or as yet undetermined problem(s) may have been the social conditions that contributed to Jenny's symptoms.

Thinking in terms of behavioral metaphors permits the therapist to gain a better understanding of the child's problem in the family context. Just as a literary metaphor gives the reader an understanding of a new concept or idea, a behavioral metaphor helps the observer understand a specific social situation. Jenny's symptoms, considered as a behavioral metaphor, represented someone's inability to step forward or move without pain. My task was to develop a hypothesis about the cause of the problem in terms of metaphor. Who was represented by the behavioral metaphor? What situation was represented by the behavioral metaphor? What series of interactions was represented by the behavioral metaphor?

With the information Ray had provided thus far, I tentatively hypothesized that the parent's marital difficulties were a very important consideration in understanding Jenny's situation. The parents had been separated and living on opposite coasts for a year. I thought that leaving her husband had been a painful step for Jenny's mother, since Jenny's painful steps had begun shortly after the separation. However, her mother, for some reason, would not or could not move back to rejoin her husband.

Ray did not have any information about the relationship between the mother and grandmother or about the family's response to the grandfather's death. All of the parents' individual and marital problems may have been solvable; however, their living on opposite coasts provided little opportunity for problem resolution. Before developing a therapeutic plan, I had to know why the mother would not return to her husband. Had she already decided on a divorce? Was she involved in another relationship? Was she worried about her widowed mother? I called Ray: "Ray, you need to find out why Jenny's mother is not willing to rejoin her husband to resolve their problems."

The Therapist's View

Barbara had explained that I should think of the problem of Jenny's immobility not as originating within Jenny's psyche but as representative of another problem. My goal for the next session was to uncover the missing information about Jenny's family situation. According to Barbara's directions, I thanked the parents and grandmother for coming with Jenny to the session and emphasized the importance of our working together to help Jenny focus her complete energy on healing. I asked for more details concerning various relationships and situations in the family. Notably, as the family talked about the grandfather's death, I discovered that the grandfather had engaged Jenny's mother in a deathbed promise to care for the grandmother. Mother and grandmother talked and cried about grandfather in a fond way, clearly missing and loving him.

The other thing that Barbara asked me to do during this information-gathering session was to have Jenny sit between her parents while they reassured Jenny that every problem would be handled by them alone and that Jenny was to devote 100% of her energy to the rehabilitation of her legs. She was notably excited and smiling, and appeared to be quite content sitting between the two of them.

Process

The Supervisor's View

"A deathbed promise! That's it," I thought. Jenny's mother can't leave her own mother because she promised her father on his deathbed that she would care for her. And how could she care for her mother if she reconciled with her husband and returned to the opposite coast? Although the parents had marital problems and problems with depression and alcohol, the grandfather's death had risen to the surface as the primary social-situation problem. The mother's deathbed promise prevented her from rejoining her husband, thus precluding any solution of their marital problems. I could now better understand Jenny's leg pain. The pain that prevented her from walking initially represented her mother's pain in leaving her husband, and now was expanded to represent her inability to move forward because of the emotional pain that would be caused by violating the deathbed promise. Jenny was immobilized by her painful steps, and her mother was immobilized by the emotional pain her departure would have caused her own mother.

Ray now had one more session with the family while Jenny's father was still in town, which meant I had to develop for him a one-session cure that would (a) relieve Jenny's symptoms, (b) release her mother from the deathbed promise, (c) ensure the grandmother's welfare, and (d) bring the parents together to solve their marital problems.

I gave the following directives to Ray to engineer our one-session cure.

1. Ray should invite Jenny's grandmother to the next day's session. Although she was going through a grieving process and did have some minor health problems, Ray described her as being physically and emotionally self-sufficient. I said to explain to her during the session that although the doctors were uncertain about the cause of Jenny's physical symptoms they felt certain that the mind and body work very closely together. When Jenny's mind is preoccupied with worries about her family, she has less energy available for the physical healing process. The emphasis should be that Jenny needs 100% of her emotional energy to focus on her physical healing.

   He should explain to Jenny's grandmother that it is impossible for her daughter to return to her husband to resolve their marital difficulties because of the deathbed promise she has made to her father. He should simply ask the grandmother whether she needs her daughter to remain at her home to care for her. If she says no, which was my assumption, he should ask her to hold her daughter's hand and release her from the deathbed promise to look after her. He should direct the grandmother as she tells her daughter, "I understand the promise you made to your father was because you both love me, but you don't need to sacrifice your life and marriage for my sake." He should have Jenny's grandmother state in no uncertain terms that she is perfectly capable of caring for herself.

2. To ensure the grandmother's welfare and the mother's peace of mind, Ray should make certain that the mother's sister, who lived in the same town,

would care for the grandmother. He should ask Jenny's mother to talk to her sister privately and in detail about whether she would accept the responsibility of caring for their mother, a responsibility she had assured her father that she, herself, would accept.

3. Once Jenny's mother felt released from the deathbed promise, the parents would need a plan for how they would reconcile. I told Ray to direct the parents to go to a place in the area that had been important to them during their courtship, make a three-month plan for their lives, and communicate that plan to Jenny. It was my belief that once released from the deathbed promise, Jenny's mother would plan to return to her husband and attempt a reconciliation. And once her mother was able to leave Jenny's grandmother, Jenny's psychosomatic symptoms, I believed, would stop.

4. If the parents decided to reunite on the opposite coast, Ray should recommend that they immediately seek marital therapy. He should assure them that he would refer them to someone who would continue the work that he had begun. He and I agreed that we would go to any lengths to find a therapist on the opposite coast who had a strategic point of view.

The Therapist's View

At the second and final session that Jenny's father could attend before his departure, I had to effectively implement the directives that Barbara had proposed (what pressure!). I wrote all of the directives Barbara had given me on 3-by-5-inch note cards and put them in my pocket. This was a serious case and a new procedure that I did not intend to bungle. This is what transpired.

1. Although Jenny's grandmother contended that her daughter did not remain with her because of the deathbed promise (something I would have believed had I not consulted with Barbara), she did understand the importance of absolving her daughter of her promise. She said she wanted her daughter to be happy and to work on her marriage. They held hands, cried, and recalled grandfather's love that had prompted the promise. Jenny's grandmother reassured her daughter that she could care for herself.

2. Jenny's mother agreed to seek her sister's help in monitoring her mother's health and happiness.

3. The parents had been talking about how they had grown up, met, and dated in the area, so I asked them to go to a place that was meaningful in their courtship to talk about a three-month plan for their lives. During the session they were turned toward each other, and they continually looked at each other. It was my belief that they had no intention of separating and that they were still very much attached to one another.

4. I told the parents that if they chose to reunite on the opposite coast for the purpose of reconciliation I would make certain they were referred to an excellent marital therapist.

Outcome

The Therapist's View

When Jenny, her mother, her grandmother, and two of the other children came to my office one week later, I was amazed. Jenny walked into the room without crutches! She was limping slightly but was able to apply weight to her leg. She reported that her pain level had dropped by 50% and she looked 100% better! Jenny appeared happier and reported that she had played with her cousins and even played in the swimming pool without feeling much pain in her foot.

Jenny's mother reported that she and Jenny's father had gone to a state park, where they had spent romantic times during their courtship, and discussed their marital and financial problems. When her father returned to the West Coast, the couple had an undefined plan for the future but had thoroughly discussed their difficulties. Jenny appeared to be somewhat oblivious, at least overtly, to the specifics that were being discussed. However, as evidenced by her new posture and stance in life, she was very aware that there had been changes in her family.

I asked Jenny's mother if she would encourage weekly contact between the children and father by providing writing supplies and stamps. Although the father's depression was never addressed, I was sure that he missed his family and that he would certainly feel better if he had constant communication with them.

Another session was scheduled, but the family did not come or call. I phoned soon after the missed appointment and Jenny's mother stated that Jenny was doing well and was not experiencing any pain. She also reported that she and her husband had decided to get back together and she was preparing to move the children back to the family home.

Later, I saw the referring doctor in the hallway and mentioned Jenny's progress. He was pleased but not nearly as excited or impressed as I was. But then, this was a doctor who felt psychology had no function in our society. The occupational and physical therapy staffs were also very pleased, but each felt that their interventions explained Jenny's progress. Overall, I was very depressed that I was not getting the recognition I wanted and felt I deserved. Being a therapist, I was beginning to understand, was not going to be an easy task. Barbara was clear in her direction that I should give the credit for Jenny's improvement to the family, as they were the ones who helped her the most.

When I spoke to the family two years later by phone, I learned that Jenny had not had any recurring symptoms and was doing well, and the parents were still together. They had not received any other therapy, although I had given them the name of a therapist in their city.

Five years after this case I find myself immersed in the strategies and theory of brief therapies, especially strategic family therapy. My thinking has completely shifted from a one-person, psychodynamic orientation to a systems perspective that enables me to think of problem situations and conditions in an entirely different way. I look for the causes of problem behavior in the social situation, rather than in the individual. Jenny and her mother have stepped forward in life without pain, and I have stepped forward in my understanding of human behavior with excitement!

The Supervisor's View

It was a relief to hear that Jenny's symptoms had abated by 50% in one week's time. This was an indication that the strategies developed to change the organization of Jenny's social situation were appropriate and that she most likely would recover very quickly. We can never be certain what directive or combination of directives began the change that included the remission of Jenny's symptoms. We can only surmise in this situation that Jenny's pain and her inability to take steps were lessened as her mother confronted her own pain over leaving her husband and her anticipated pain over leaving her mother.

The rapid remission of symptoms also spoke well of Ray's therapeutic skill and his ability to shift to a new style of therapy for the benefit of a client. He did not have to completely understand the theory to successfully implement the strategies of the method. The success that Ray experienced with Jenny and her family prompted him to ask for further supervision in cases in which he could apply strategic family therapy. Jenny's case began a professional relationship between us that moved in five years from that of supervisor and supervisee to that of friend and colleague.

Discussion

As the supervisor in the case, when I was thinking about what interventions would help relieve Jenny's painful symptoms, I looked for elements in Jenny's social context that if changed would make her symptoms unnecessary. The strategic problem solver assumes that at the point a child presents a symptom the family unit (i.e., the social situation) has become immobilized in regard to a larger problem than is presented through the child. The child's problem is a metaphor for the larger problem, and it has a protective or helpful function in the interactions of the family in that it serves as a diversion.

Once the larger social-situation problem is tentatively identified—in this case the deathbed promise that prevented Jenny's mother and father from being together to solve their marital problems—the therapist can design interventions that will solve the larger problem, eliminating the cause of the child's problem. The interventions are presented to the family in the form of directives with the rationale that they will solve the child's problem. In this case, Jenny's grandmother was asked to release Jenny's mother from the deathbed promise she had made because Jenny, Ray believed, was worried and upset about her parents' separation and her mother could not rejoin her father because of the promise.

The directive that asked the parents to make a three-month plan for their lives was also presented with the rationale of helping Jenny. If her doubts and uncertainties about the future were relieved, she could concentrate her mental and physical energy on healing. Having Jenny's mother ask her sister to accept primary responsibility for their mother's care would give Jenny's mother peace of mind and allow her to focus her mental and physical energy on restoring her marriage.

The strategic approach to family therapy makes use of a planned problem-solving strategy for each case. Although some standard strategies are commonly used for solving problem situations, the strategic therapist strives to design interventions based on the particular social situation that seems to be the source of the presenting problem. Rather than attempt to change the individual, the therapist designs a plan to change the conditions, interactions, or relationships that exist in the individual's surrounding environment.

References

American Psychiatric Association. (2000). *Diagnostic and statistical manual of mental disorders: DSM-IV-TR* (4th ed., text revision). Washington, DC: Author.

Haley, J. (1980). *Leaving home*. New York: McGraw-Hill.

Madanes, C. (1981). *Strategic family therapy*. San Francisco: Jossey-Bass.

Peeks, B. (1989). "Strategies for solving children's problems understood as behavioral metaphors," *Journal of Strategic and Systemic Therapies, 8*(1), 22–25.

Biographical Statements

Barbara Peeks Dunn, MS, is a family therapist in private practice, who also works as an elementary school counselor with Lincoln Public Schools in Lincoln, Nebraska. She teaches and publishes systemic problem solving in the context of schools and conducts workshops for agencies and school districts nationwide. You can reach Barbara at bjpeeks@aol.com.

Ray L. Levy, PhD, received his bachelor of arts degree from Harvard University in 1979. He then attended Virginia Commonwealth University, where he received both his master's and doctoral degrees in clinical psychology. He completed his internship at the Dallas Child Guidance Clinic. Ray is currently in private practice in Dallas, where he works in a solution-oriented style and specializes in treating children and adolescents. Ray has also written *Try and Make Me!* with Bill O'Hanlon, a book about parenting strong-willed children (Rodale Press). You can reach Ray at levyporter@aol.com.

CHAPTER 11

Ringo: Scars of Violence

Vimala Pillari

Vimala Pillari attempts to intervene with 12-year-old Larry who has been horribly disfigured both physically and emotionally. Although the diagnosis of Larry's violent behavior as Conduct Disorder (DSM-IV-TR) is accurate, it is also an understatement.

Pillari brings us a case from early in her career. She brings love and consistency to the chaotic existence of her institutionalized client. Larry responds with impressive behavioral gains. A dramatic encounter between Larry and his estranged mother Sadie illustrates both the tenacity and hurtfulness of a relationship that has been scarred by catastrophic violence.

Twelve-year-old Larry was referred to me for acting-out behaviors while I was a part-time therapist in a publicly funded residential treatment center for emotionally disturbed children. Larry, born into a lower socioeconomic family, was the youngest of six siblings. Sadie, Larry's mother, had not finished high school. She worked off and on as a maid. Larry's oldest sister was married and lived close to her mother's house. Three of his brothers were living away from home. One of them had been hospitalized for three weeks for "mental problems." One teenage sister continued to live at home with her mother. Allen, Larry's father, was serving a life prison sentence. Larry had not seen his father since he was 6 years old.

Larry had lived in this residential treatment center for the past three years. He had been expelled from school because of uncontrolled violent behavior. The courts placed him in the center because his behavior had culminated in an incident in which he was found choking a classmate until the victim literally turned blue in the face. To make matters worse, Larry joked about his violent acts and did not understand the seriousness of hurting others.

Sadie had dropped him off three years before as if he were going to a boarding school. She did not tell him that the facility was a residential center for children with serious behavioral disorders. All of my attempts to get in touch with her had proved futile.

Conceptualization

Based on the *DSM-IV-TR* diagnostic framework, Larry was labeled as having a Conduct Disorder. This was a common diagnosis for children in our setting who typically displayed acting-out behaviors that made it difficult for them to live at home.

The approaches I used to work with Larry varied from cognitive-behavioral to psychodynamic. Psychodynamic and family systems theory influenced my assessment and planning for Larry. Essentially, I used my relationship with Larry to provide a corrective emotional experience. I set limits in order to promote constructive, acceptable behavior.

Process

By the time I had joined the staff, Larry had been in residence for three years. The first day I met Larry was memorable. I had just enough time to admire the beautiful view of the river through the window in my new office before the peace was shattered by repeated shouts of, "So you are my new counselor." By the time I looked up from a record I was reading, he had slammed the door and was gone. But he was back in a few minutes banging on my door, barging in and out, and repeating with exaggerated sarcasm, "So you are my new counselor." Larry did this a number of times, to my great embarrassment, for I was aware of the presence of other social workers who could not help but overhear this unpleasant commotion.

When he barged in for the fifth time, I demanded, attempting to be reality oriented, that he not bang on my door and said that if he had anything to say he should walk in politely and talk to me directly. To my horror, he doubled over and burst into loud screeching laughter: "You're crazee . . . crazee . . . and you are not supposed to get angry at me. We are crazy kids and you are supposed to be kind and understanding towards us always." With this interesting and somewhat insightful commentary he was, thankfully, gone. My face felt hot as I self-consciously thought of the impression made on my senior colleagues. Of course, in time, I found out that every worker had occasional uproar to contend with in this setting.

Half an hour later, in walked Larry. This time he made his declaration in an amused and triumphant manner: "So you are my new counselor!" I was alert as he moved closer to my desk. Except for a slit through which he could see, Larry's face was covered with the hood of his coat. I asked his name and he responded. I requested that I be allowed to see his face. He hesitated and I persuaded. Finally, he unzipped his hood slowly, revealing his forehead, his brown eyes, and his nose. Then, in a flash he unzipped the hood, and I got a glimpse of his mouth before he zipped it back. What a sight! There was a large scar around his lips, apparently the result of a burn. His lower lip was double the size of the upper. Ignoring my attempts to start a conversation, Larry moved to the window. Seeing that it was closed, he asked if he could open it. It was a winter morning and cold outside.

Counselor:	Please don't.
Larry:	Why not?
Counselor:	It's cold outside.
Larry:	You cannot open the window because those are the rules. (*He spoke in a mocking tone of voice and pointed to a notice stapled on the wall.*)

I explained that I had not had a chance to read the material. He laughed raucously and ran out, faithfully slamming the door and screaming, "You are crazee!"

Though I was supposed to see Larry only twice a week, he was back in my office the next day. He mockingly greeted me, "Hello, counselor," and slammed the door. I was frustrated. How was I to deal with this youngster who made me feel so uncomfortable? Again, Larry started his running in and out of my office routine. Then he ran up and put his face almost against mine and asked if he could have the ashtray on my table. I put my hand on the ashtray and told him that he could not have it. Sensing an opportunity, I added that I did not like his slamming my door and running in and out of my office.

I thought I was "structuring" Larry. However, he commented nonchalantly, "You are not supposed to get angry with us. We are crazy, so counselors cannot get angry with us."

It seemed high time to correct this unfortunate interpretation of the rules that were governing our relationship: "Of course, you are not crazy and I'm not going to treat you as if you were," I heard myself saying. "If I'm angry, I will tell you all about it. Counselors get angry, too."

Larry ran to the door and yelled, "Crazee counselor, crazee . . . crazee . . . ," and disappeared.

Suddenly, there was a commotion in the corridor and I heard a woman scream my name. I ran out and found the new secretary, pale and shaking all over, holding her throat. Larry had tried to choke her. She was frightened. Larry looked at her and laughed and said, "I was only playing with her." For the first time, I noticed that he was very muscular for a child who was only 12.

After this incident, new rules were made for Larry's visits. Whenever Larry came to the treatment building, he had to ring for me at the door and I had to go and fetch him. Far from being disturbed by the new procedure, Larry seemed delighted with the special attention.

After the first few sessions, during which Larry (and I) learned that he could not push me around, we got down to therapy. One day I brought up the subject of his previous counselor, a man who had had to leave his job abruptly because his mother was dying in another state. Larry spoke sadly, saying that he missed the other counselor. He said that he did not like counselors because they came and left so fast. Larry's statement was true enough, and I realized that he was suffering from many losses. I attempted to talk about his mother, but he was not ready to discuss her.

I discovered that Larry had some strengths. First of all, he was quite bright and enjoyed reading. He was also musical. We talked about his interest in music. He liked playing the guitar, and he told me that one day he would like to join the band that his brother Joseph had started.

Larry was creative. He would draw pictures and tell stories. He had quite a sense of humor and loved to laugh and joke. However, his jokes were hurtful and targeted at specific people. Still, humor was a means of communication between us. I would bring the newspaper comics and we read them together. This helped both of us to relax.

I constantly drilled Larry on acceptable social behavior, presenting it as normal growing-up behavior. As Larry got comfortable with me, he stopped covering his mouth.

The kids in his cottage called him "Ringo" and sometimes taunted him by singing, "Ring around the lips." One Monday Larry came to my office with tears in his eyes. He said that he hated the boys because they were always making jokes about his lips. I asked him what had happened to give him such a scar around his lips. So, with pain and even amusement, Larry told me what had happened.

When he was perhaps 5 or 6, his parents, who were always fighting, were having an especially violent argument. Larry was scared but also thirsty. He wanted milk from the carton that his mother had placed near the stove (which was on). Perhaps, at some level, he thought that his request for milk would stop the fighting. Sadie told him not to touch the milk. He would have his milk with supper. However, Allen, taunting his wife, instructed his son to get the milk immediately and drink it. Although his father was rarely home, Larry was afraid of his bad temper. He had been beaten by both parents, but he was more afraid of his father's beatings. Larry decided he had better obey his father. So he picked up the milk carton. Sadie, in a rage, pushed Larry's face into the hot stove. It was several days before Larry received medical attention. The doctors said that nothing could be done to remove the massive scarred tissue around his lips.

Simplistically, Larry saw the scar as the cause of all his problems. He did not blame his parents. I would learn later that Larry was considered the ugly duckling in his family even prior to the scarification. It seems likely that Larry was the least favored child because he was obviously less physically attractive than his siblings. He described his mother as being beautiful.

Larry asked me if his lips could be "cured." I told him that the original medical report didn't hold out much hope. I also knew that it was unlikely that there would be funds to pay for such "elective" surgery. Nevertheless, I managed to get together sufficient support to take Larry to see a plastic surgeon. Unfortunately, the plastic surgeon did not think anything could be done. Larry was disappointed but grateful that I had taken him to the doctor.

Although I was aware that another catastrophic family incident had been responsible for the father's life imprisonment, I kept wondering about the right time to probe this subject. The opportunity presented itself as we discussed the prison system and why people go to jail. At first, as was his pattern, Larry laughed about his father being in prison, but he was soon caught up in the terrifying and anxious moments that he related to me.

As frequently happened, his father and mother were fighting, although Larry could not remember why. This time his father was drunk. Allen started to beat Sadie. Larry was scared and ran to his maternal grandmother, who was living with them at the time, and hid behind her. Allen became more violent and would not stop beating Sadie, so the grandmother intervened. Cursing and yelling, she came to her daughter's rescue and started to fight Allen. Allen picked up a butcher knife and stabbed his mother-in-law repeatedly until she fell to the kitchen floor. Larry recalled that the floor became red with blood. Petrified, Larry stood in the corner of the room. He remembered crying and his father yelling at him, and he vaguely recalled his father being taken away by the police. His grandmother died. He twitched his nose and said that he still remembered the putrid odors that lingered in the room for a long time. Larry was lost when his grandmother died because she was the only person who would stand by him.

The murder happened when Larry was 6, and that was the last time he saw his father. For a long time Larry could not sleep at night. At home he was afraid that his mother might kill him, just as his father had killed his grandmother. He had not spoken of this to anyone until now.

School was a relief in the sense that he could act out without fear of being murdered! When Larry was 9, he started getting into serious trouble at school. What he called fun was seen by others as aggressive and abusive. He beat younger kids, sometimes to the point that the other child was bloody. Larry commented that he was only playing.

A number of such incidents paved the road to this institution, where Larry arrived at age 10. He was under the impression that any kind of behavior was acceptable here because crazy kids were expected to be unpredictable.

In therapy, I highlighted Larry's strong points: verbal skills, good academic performance in school, ability to play the guitar, and successful attempts to control his behavior. In response to my caring, encouragement, and consistent limit setting, Larry's behavior began to improve markedly.

There were positive observations from staff and other children. What an ego boost for Larry! He would talk to me again and again about how his cottage parents kept telling him that he was turning out to be a fine young man. I was pleased with his progress, but I wondered where we could go from here. What were Larry's prospects as an adult?

I had been aware for a long time that music was Larry's first love, so we talked about guitar lessons and his desire to join his brother's band. I made arrangements for him to save the pocket money he earned through odd jobs at the center for guitar lessons. The agency that administered the center contributed as well. Larry took to his guitar lessons enthusiastically. Meanwhile I tried to get in touch with his oldest brother, Joseph. I hoped that Joseph would be good role model, and I helped Larry start what would be a sporadic correspondence with his brother.

While the relationship between brothers was being reinforced by telephone calls and letter writing, Larry's behavior continued to improve. After his quarterly assessment by the consulting psychiatrist, I got a telephone call. The psychiatrist was pleasantly surprised at Larry's self-controlled behavior and the manner in which he interacted. I felt very good about that call!

Larry brought up his intense desire to see his mother, Sadie, whom he had not seen in the three years since she had dropped him at the "boarding school." My attempts to get her to visit were fruitless. She would promise to come but would not keep her word. This soft-spoken woman was very elusive about her commitment to her son. I encouraged Larry to write but, of course, Sadie did not reply. He interpreted this lack of response as rejection. He would ask me, "Does my mother really hate me?"

At times, I sat by myself in my office after Larry left, trying to understand his mother's behavior. I had to admit to considerable anger toward this woman I had never met. Larry told me that he loved his mother, adding defensively that whatever a mother does to a child is all right because she was responsible for his birth. I had heard this type of logic from other abused kids.

I became almost obsessed with setting up a meeting with Sadie. Thus, I began a lengthy correspondence with her which included phone calls and letter writing. When I finally got in touch with her, she declined my invitation to visit the treatment center. Fast as lightening, I asked if we could visit her at home. Perhaps caught off guard, Sadie agreed.

Larry and I took the train and then the subway to visit her. Larry was chatty, recalling happy memories of home, mostly things he did with his grandmother and sisters. He said very little about his relationship with his parents.

Sadie lived in an old, run-down brick home. She was an attractive woman with startlingly large brown eyes. My heart sank as I realized that Larry truly had not inherited her good looks. As we walked into the house, Sadie started talking to me. There were no words of affection or hugs for Larry. She matter-of-factly asked Larry how he was doing in school.

The youngest daughter, Melanie, who was about three years older than Larry and obviously pregnant, lived at home. Although it was a school day, Melanie was at home. Melanie was engaged in various household chores, and there was ongoing arguing between mother and daughter about how these should be done. Melanie made no attempt to interact with her brother. Larry drifted to another side of the house to see his old bedroom. He loitered as he came back to the family room, obviously uncomfortable.

Later, Sadie invited me into the kitchen. Calling out to Larry, she offered us milk to drink. Larry did not want any and I declined as well. Sadie took a swig straight from the milk carton and replaced it in the refrigerator. She did this a number of times, bringing to mind an empty container trying desperately and vainly to fill itself.

I asked about her other children. She seemed particularly proud of her oldest son Joseph, the musician. I interrupted to say that Larry had been corresponding with Joseph. I added that he was learning to play the guitar and would eventually like to join his brother's band. Sadie looked at Larry, rolled her eyes upward and sighed, as if to say, "I can't imagine a loser like Larry playing in Joseph's band." Could her disregard for Larry be based on something so superficial as looks?

Trying to be constructive, I asked Sadie if she had any plans for Larry's future, particularly after he returned home. Now I saw pain and anger written all over her face. In an anguished voice she told me that trouble began in her marriage only after Larry's birth. She saw Larry as an "evil" child, though he could not help it "because he was born that way." She told me that Larry looked and acted "ugly" from birth. I told Sadie about Larry's behavioral improvements at the center. She was silent.

As we were leaving, Sadie put her head out the window and yelled to Larry that he could come and live with her when he had a job.

Larry and I walked briskly to the train station. I was in no mood to discuss the visit. My thoughts about Sadie were not pleasant, and, of course, I didn't want to share them with Larry. I was worried that Larry would act out right there on the train. I wondered if I had done the right thing in taking Larry to visit his mother. Was it useful and important for Larry to know where he stood with his mother? Sadie would never accept him unless, perhaps, he brought money. Was rejection ever helpful to children?

Larry clung to Sadie's parting words. She must love him if she wanted him to come home after he found a job.

In spite of this miserable meeting, I hoped that more communication would follow. I invited Sadie to parent education meetings, promising her round-trip train fare, but she declined.

Following the home visit, as I expected and feared, Larry started to act out in the residential cottage as well as in school. His behavior deteriorated. Thus I was aware that, at some level, Larry was conscious of Sadie's rejection. Larry got into trouble in school and did everything possible in a negative way to get my attention. He threw temper tantrums with teachers and his cottage parents and got into fistfights with other boys. I waited out the storm and stuck by him. It took two full months for Larry to get back the discipline and self-control he had achieved prior to the home visit.

In our staff meetings, we discussed what could be done for Larry when he became a young adult. Eventually, we made plans to send Larry, when he was older, to a group home for independent living if he was not able to go home. I diligently worked at sustaining the relationship between Larry and his older brother Joseph. I encouraged Larry to call Joseph and invite him to come for a visit. Joseph did come and, thankfully, the interaction was positive. Joseph encouraged Larry in his schoolwork and musical aspirations. I believe that this visit was one of the best gifts Larry had ever received!

There were other issues that were unresolved. One included my inability to do anything about his relationship with his father, whom he had not seen since he was about 6 years old. The absence of his father was one of the biggest gaps in Larry's life. His father would be ready for parole in another five years. The fact that his relationship with his mother did not progress was another serious issue. I tried to work on this with Larry by pointing out that all people have frailties, including his mother, who had her own set of problems to face and did not seem ready for a relationship with Larry. He continued to defend his mother's behavior. A number of sessions were spent helping Larry understand and accept the fact that he could not reestablish a relationship with Sadie until she was ready.

Outcome and Discussion

My final sessions with Larry were painful for me. I could not change Larry's role in the family as the most disliked child. I could not provide the love he had missed. I could not repair his scarred face.

I resigned from the treatment center to pursue my doctorate in social work. Larry was passed on to another counselor. Later, I was able to find out only that he eventually "left" the agency. The social service system has a short memory; there are too many needy people standing in line.

My skin has grown thicker with experience. I wanted to share this case from a point in time when I may have overinvested in my clients. Certainly, I was deeply touched by the personality of this particular child.

Reference

American Psychiatric Association. (2000). *Diagnostic and statistical manual of mental disorders: DSM-IV-TR* (4th ed., text revision). Washington, DC: Author.

Biographical Statement

Vimala Pillari, DSW, is Dean, Graduate School of Social Work, Dominican University, Illinois. Her recent books are *Shadows of Pain: Intimacy and Sexual Problems in Family Life, Human Behavior in the Social Environment I and II,* and *Models of Family Therapy.* You can reach Vimala at vpillari@email.dom.edu.

CHAPTER 12

A Peaceful Solution

Kirk Zinck and John M. Littrell

Kirk Zinck is brought in to a junior high school to resolve a potentially violent conflict between two teenage girls and their "camp followers." Zinck uses solution-focused brief counseling and peer-centered conflict resolution as he plants positive suggestions and empowers his clients to take steps on their own behalf. Zinck pays careful attention to language as a means to reframe situations and thereby encourage the belief that change can be rapid, incremental, and progressive. The work is completed in three sessions. E-mail made possible a consultative relationship between Zinck in Alaska and John Littrell in Iowa, especially in the conceptualization and writing stages of this case.

The seven-month old strife revolving around three eighth-grade students—Jennifer, Anna, and Cody—showed no signs of abating. The original conflict had mushroomed to include other students, who amplified the dispute in hallways, classrooms, and common areas.

I am a high-school counselor in an Alaskan community where there is also a junior high school. The junior-high-school principal asked for my assistance. According to her, the conflict had defeated school administrators and counselors, teachers, and parents. It is touchy being called from one school to intervene in another as an "expert." In this situation, I had positive and long-standing relationships with many of the staff at that school and experience in conflict resolution and anger management.

The overcrowded 700-student junior high draws from a population of middle- and low-income families. Low-cost and low-income housing as well as commercial development surrounds the school. Crime, family dysfunction, and abuse contribute to a tense and sometimes dangerous community. Some long-term resident families with generations of family abuse and between-family conflicts live in the neighbor-hood. In the school, conflict can be especially difficult to resolve because fighting is a normal occurrence in the students' daily lives.

The principal gave me a history of the conflict. Anna and Jennifer were insep-arable friends at the time they joined the cheerleading squad in a summer soccer league. They shared the typical activities of teenagers, including intense conversa-tions, hanging out at each other's homes, and listening to the rock music they both enjoyed. Anna's family was trouble-ridden and Anna confided in Jennifer's parents. Jennifer's parents tried to be helpful to Anna.

Anna's mother sponsored the summer cheerleading squad. Jennifer, attractive and popular, attracted the attention of the boys and Anna became jealous. Then Anna's mother kicked Jennifer off the squad. Jennifer replaced Anna with a friendship with another classmate, Cody. Conflict between Anna and Jennifer intensified and drew in Cody.

Resumption of school in the eighth grade provided fertile ground for the con-flict. Jennifer and Cody were average students, involved in sports and other school activities. They were liked by teachers and admired by peers. Anna was a poor student due to poor attendance, yet she was intelligent, outgoing, and tough. She at-tracted friends whose lives were in turmoil and who looked to her as a leader. Thus, as students became aware of the conflict, they took sides. This alignment brought attention, excitement, and group membership. Some encouraged the conflict by car-rying messages and rumors, while others actively intimidated and fought. As the strife escalated, safety needs became paramount. Each side was involving more students and adults in an attempt to provide protection and to intimidate. Threats increased. Jennifer and Cody were scared and tried to avoid confrontations.

The flexing of power was a critical element in this confrontation. Both Anna and Jennifer enlisted girls and even a few boys who were called on to back them. As more students got pulled in, there was more potential for someone to get hurt physically.

The involvement of adults provided the combatants with a sense of power and, paradoxically, took away power. In their attempts to manage the conflict, school officials and parents took responsibility for resolving it away from the participants. Nor did the adults have much success.

Anna's mother fueled the conflict and effectively neutralized efforts by the school staff. She threatened her daughter with removal from school if Anna did not fight Jennifer and Cody. Anna's mother actually offered money to any student who would beat up her daughter's two antagonists. There were frequent and heated disputes with school staff and on one occasion, Anna's mother angrily confronted Jennifer's parents at school.

Further complicating the situation was the involvement of a small gang of teens from other schools who aligned behind Anna. During an outdoor physical education class, one of the gang arrived at the field with gasoline, matches, and a knife. Her alleged plan was to cut Jennifer's hair off and set her on fire! A teacher intervened before the assault took place.

Anna's mother was chronically unemployed and frequently hospitalized for psychiatric problems. Although Anna's grandparents filled in as much as they could,

Anna was often unsupervised. Her gang affiliation and leadership filled some of the social and familial void. In contrast, Jennifer came from an intact and close family. Jennifer's parents filed assault charges against Anna and some members of her gang after a confrontation at a movie theater. It didn't help.

Cody came from a poverty-stricken household and her mother was partially disabled and a single parent. Peers teased her about her family circumstances. Keeping the friendship with Jennifer and her family was extremely important to Cody, as they provided a secure environment.

Months of dealing with this conflict had exhausted the resources of school personnel and was tearing the student body apart. Worse, when a male administrator met with all three to mediate the conflict, Anna accused him of sexually molesting her. The allegation proved to be false. Anna had a tendency to bolt dramatically from the room whenever the conversation went against her. Understandably, school personnel became discouraged about any positive intervention. Following yet another suspension for fighting, Anna refused to return to school. However, she continued to call out "her girls" to intimidate Jennifer and Cody.

Well, that was the scene when the principal asked me to talk with the three students. She wanted me to use a methodical, step-by-step process to defuse conflict. I agreed to work with the students, but insisted on my own approach. I believed that the principal's approach would be too time-consuming in a crisis demanding fast de-escalation. In addition, I had limited professional time to devote to this case. I resolved to make this crisis a test case for solution-focused therapy combined with peer-centered conflict resolution.

Conceptualization

In this section, John Littrell and I propose a diagnosis for each of the three students. Then we discuss the solution-focused brief counseling model and a peer-centered conflict resolution approach.

Diagnosis

Solely to address the interests of the reader, we are providing a formal diagnosis for each client. We do not recommend that school counselors formally diagnose students. Few schools offer an appropriate clinical setting and most school counselors are not adequately trained in assessment. More to the point, the *DSM-IV-TR* is poorly suited for use with families and groups.

The *DSM-IV-TR* diagnosis for Jennifer and Cody is Adjustment Disorder. Anxiety precipitated by the threat posed by Anna and her friends was the underlying stressor. We would specify "acute" and expect that the symptoms would disappear upon cessation of the conflict. The disturbance of conduct was a situational and defensive response.

Anna is entitled to a somewhat more severe diagnosis. I would prefer Conduct Disorder (Provisional). The "provisional" tag indicates that although I expected the disorder to meet all of the criteria for Conduct Disorder, I felt the need for more information regarding Anna's activities. As a *DSM-IV-TR* diagnosis was not important to treatment, I chose not to go back to confirm a "repetitive and persistent pattern" of misbehavior. From a systemic perspective, Anna's antisocial behaviors may have met basic emotional needs that were seldom satisfied in her family life.

Solution-Focused Brief Counseling

I work in a public school where long-term counseling is unrealistic. Through an ongoing process of attending workshops and seminars, reading, practice, and then teaching the approach to other counselors, I have become a solution-focused brief counselor. Solution-focused brief counseling is the best counseling model I've found for such a setting. I base my work on the Mental Research Institute (MRI) four-step model of brief counseling (Fisch, Weakland, & Segal, 1982; Watzlawick, Weakland, & Fisch, 1974) plus solution-focused modifications adapted from the work of de Shazer (1988; DeJong & Berg, 1998; Littrell, 1998).

Step 1. Define the problem in behavioral terms.

Step 2. Look for past actions that might serve as a foundation for constructing present solutions. Anna and Jennifer had once been friends. I would build on past success.

Step 3. Select small and manageable goals. Adolescents are visual and receptive to indirect suggestions. I like to use the "video technique," in which the client describes her behavior as if watching herself on TV. The video technique helps with internal rehearsal and reinforcement and enables the client to imaginatively edit the action. The video becomes a creative act of scripting in accord with the client's goals and ideal self-image.

Step 4. Set achievable tasks to help the clients reach their goals. The tasks should provide immediate and observable success. It helps to find supportive peers, family members, or teachers who will comment on any changes they observe.

Language techniques are useful in all of the four steps to (a) normalize problems, (b) reframe situations in order to open up more choices, and (c) encourage the belief that change can be rapid, incremental, and progressive. For example, the counselor might say, "I wonder if change will start immediately or if it will take a few days before we see it?"

Peer-Centered Conflict Resolution

The basic idea is that young people are helped to reach mutually beneficial agreements that will result in a resolution of a conflict. It is more effective if students solve conflicts at the peer level. Conflict consumes energy, and eventually people tire of it and seek either avoidance or resolution. As long as adults expend their resources, the combatants can retain a reserve of energy to keep the conflict going.

Process

I arranged our meetings in the conference room of a community recreation center not far from the school. I wanted a neutral place that would provide a sense of significance and also be less vulnerable to the student grapevine. The principal provided the students with transportation.

Initial Session

Anna, who had been suspended from school, agreed to meet but failed to appear at the initial session. We later learned that Anna and her mother were undecided as to whether she would return to school for the remainder of the year. Therefore, Anna had little incentive to participate. Despite Anna's absence, I decided to proceed.

Jennifer and Cody arrived, giggling nervously and hiding in their winter coats, hands securely tucked in pockets. To counter any possibility of a repeated accusation of inappropriate touch, the school nurse was present. I explained her role as that of a neutral observer. The nurse sat outside of our circle. Because she was familiar and trusted, the students expressed no concern regarding her presence. I asked Jennifer and Cody to explain their understanding of the purpose of our meeting. They stated that the meeting was to assist them in resolving their conflict with Anna and her friends. We established that they were voluntary participants. The limits of confidentiality were discussed and they agreed to the ground rules: (1) to listen to whoever was speaking and to wait before commenting until the speaker was finished; (2) to avoid put-downs of anyone, present or not; (3) to say that they wished to "pass" if they did not want to respond to a question or statement; and (4) to keep what was said in the room confidential, with the exception that they were encouraged to discuss our meetings with their parents.

I established that a break could be requested and that leaving the room would be considered a request for a break, after which we would reconvene in five minutes. Although Anna was not present, I wanted to anticipate "bolting." Thus, this norm would be established already.

We talked about what a resolution of the conflict might look like. Jennifer said, "You would see us talking together in the halls and you wouldn't see anyone calling each other names or threatening someone." Both expressed fear of Anna and her friends, but were even more afraid of Anna's mother. They anxiously asked if parents would be involved in the sessions.

To lighten things up, I asked Jennifer and Cody to tell me about things that made them laugh and happy memories they shared. As they told stories related to their friendship, they began to relax. Jennifer removed her coat and placed her forearms on the table. Cody, more timid and tense, left her coat on.

I asked what I would see if I were watching the conflict in action.

Jennifer: You would see Anna's friends come up to me in the hall and say, "Anna is going to kick your ass." Then I would go looking through the halls for Anna to threaten her back and to call her names.

Cody added that Anna's gang made threatening phone calls and had tried to intimidate them at a movie theater. Accusations that Jennifer and Cody were "talking trash" about Anna or her friends fed the conflict. We explored solutions that had been attempted or suggested, including mediation attempts by school staff members. Jennifer's father had suggested that they avoid Anna and her friends. Jennifer and Cody thought that this was good advice but it hadn't worked.

Most adolescents want to be seen as mature. I asked Jennifer and Cody if they preferred for me to address them as "girls" or as "young women." As expected, they asked to be addressed as young women. We talked about what this meant to them. I asked the "young women" to contrast how a child and a mature adult might handle conflict. I asked them to reflect upon how adults they knew handled conflicts. This strategy works when at least one significant adult in the young person's life has been available to model positive qualities. My questioning led to alternative ways of dealing with conflict, such as by moving away from potential conflict, ignoring provocative remarks, and requesting assistance of adults if threatened.

Because there were physical threats, a safety plan was developed. Unsafe places, associations, and practices were defined. On a temporary basis, Jennifer agreed to be accompanied by her parents when going to unsafe places, such as the movies, and to ignore provocations. The two would go to hockey games because Anna and company were unlikely to be there. A simple technique to discourage threatening telephone callers was adopted: if such a call is received, immediately hang up and unplug the phone for thirty minutes.

I asked, "Who do you prefer to make decisions about your lives, you or others?" Their preference for making their own decisions gave me the leverage to challenge the practice of using others to carry messages between combatants. I defined the messengers as "brokers" who incite action for the entertainment value to themselves and the power they feel in controlling a situation.

Counselor:	Who are the brokers who keep this conflict going?
Jennifer:	Well, Shane keeps telling me things that Anna says about me.
Counselor:	What does Shane get out of this?
Jennifer:	He likes to see people fight.
Counselor:	Then who is in control when Shane brings you a message?

Using the "video technique," the two young women began to visualize alternatives to fighting and to rehearse new behaviors. I used indirect suggestions to plant the idea that mature people have real alternatives by acting with forethought instead of being impulsive. Two ways to express such indirect suggestions are (1) mutual brainstorming, e.g., "I wonder what would happen if . . . ?" and (2) dropping a suggestion and then negating it, e.g., "What if . . . ? No, forget that. It was just a suggestion." I also wanted to put forward the solution-focused view that small changes spur even more and greater changes. In this session, I initiated small changes in perception and behavior with the belief that these would have a ripple effect.

I tried to get support from significant others by asking, "Who will be the first person who will notice and comment on a change?" Usually, youngsters identify someone who has stature in their eyes. Jennifer's parents were genuinely respected by the students and the school staff. I advised Jennifer and Cody to seek them out for guidance.

The session concluded with an agreement to meet again in two weeks and to include Anna, if possible. I assigned open-ended homework. Each participant was asked to consider what we had discussed in the session. Also, I asked each to agree that if she encountered conflict that she would do something *different*—something creative that hadn't been tried.

I suggested to the principal and nurse that they would probably observe "certain changes" in the days ahead. Hopefully, this suggestion would be a self-fulfilling prophecy.

Second Session

Anna attended the second session. The principal had informed her that the initial meeting had taken place. Why did she attend? My assumption is that Anna's curiosity was piqued and no one likes being left out of the action. Another positive development was that Anna told the principal that she wanted to stay in school.

Anna arrived at the second session with a positive attitude. She knew that if the conflict continued, she could be suspended or even expelled. I didn't question her regarding what had changed. I reviewed the ground rules. I decided to focus on the major participants, Jennifer and Anna. Since Cody wanted to end the conflict, I knew she would support any progress we made.

I explored with Jennifer and Anna the fun they had once shared. Jennifer and Anna talked about several hilarious phone conversations during their friendship and we were all laughing. Building on these positive feelings, I jumped to the present and asked if there had been times in the past month when they were able to get along. They told of episodes during which they were able to successfully ignore each other. In other words, they had been able to manage their conflict.

I repeated the "maturity versus childishness" ploy. Anna, as had Jennifer and Cody, welcomed the idea of being regarded as mature. I turned the discussion to those who "broker" conflicts by carrying messages. They agreed to refuse to listen to the messenger. As they shared information, it became obvious that the brokers often lied.

The video technique was used throughout the session. For example, "If someone were reviewing a videotape of the two of you getting along next week, what would they see?" and "How will you be feeling as you walk away from a friendly conversation?" My hope is that such questions create a motivating vision.

Another technique I used was to offer the "illusion" of alternatives, offering an apparent choice that reinforces the expectation that a goal will be accomplished. For example, "When do you feel this conflict will be resolved? Will it be today, tomorrow, or will it be early next week?" For good or worse, adolescents are highly suggestible. These solution-focused questions create momentum to fulfill an unspoken contract.

Throughout the initial portion of our second session, the three had huddled in their coats and slumped in their chairs. I knew we were getting somewhere when they leaned into the conversation and shed their coats.

Counselor:	Anna, will you return to school today, tomorrow, or Monday?
Anna:	I'll come on Monday.

| Counselor: | I'm impressed with how you all have handled this. I really don't have to be here. As young adults, you can settle differences by yourselves. Would you like time to talk alone, without me? |

They agreed to try. Before leaving the room, I reviewed the norms and made an individual agreement with each student to leave the room if she felt the urge to hit. If an unresolvable disagreement arose, they could ask me to rejoin them. Playfully, I told them not to break the furniture. The furniture was heavy and solid.

The nurse and I remained outside the door in case something awful happened and the principal arrived to take them back to school.

Principal:	Where are the girls?
Counselor:	The three young women are talking alone in the conference room.
Principal:	But isn't that risky?
Counselor:	Well, I told them to leave the furniture intact.
Principal:	If you say so.

After 15 minutes. I entered the room with the principal and nurse to end the session. I asked the students if they had any questions or comments.

| Jennifer: | What will happen when our friends try to start up a fight? |
| Counselor: | I'm not sure, but wouldn't it be fun to see their faces if, before they have a chance to say anything, you say, "My friend Anna is coming back to school next week." Can you imagine their reactions! |

All of us laughed. When asked if there were anything else that we needed to discuss before we adjourned, Anna stated that she would call off her gang who had been harassing Jennifer and Cody. This was a major step.

As a final note, I said that I thought that our two sessions had been productive and asked if they wished to schedule another. The students thought that another session was unnecessary. I told them that if they felt a need for a "tune-up," I would return. I explained that a tune-up would keep things running smoothly and didn't mean that the entire process had broken down. My intent was to nourish a positive expectation, while acknowledging that the going could be rough.

In a discussion with the principal the following week, she told me that Anna had returned to school, as agreed. There had been no flare-ups. "Kirk, the most amazing thing happened on the way back to school from the meeting. When I drove them over to the meeting they were silent, even hostile. When Anna touched a door knob, Jennifer made sure not to touch the same one. On the return trip, they were talking and laughing. When we got back to school, I saw Jennifer and Cody help Anna open her new locker."

Third and Final Session

Two weeks after the second session, the principal called me because Anna, Cody, and Jennifer had requested another session, so I scheduled the session at their school. They told me that they were looking forward to going to high school together next year. The conflict had become a non-issue.

I learned that Anna had developed a new friendship while Jennifer and Cody were going separate ways. Jennifer and Anna had occasional hallway conversations. Jennifer told some students that her friend, Anna, was returning to school. Anna reported a smooth reentry.

I decided against either cheering or adding new tasks and kept the meeting short. I did not expect to hear from the young women again and I have not been approached for further help.

Outcome

Seven months later, the principal reported that the former combatants had completed the remaining 10 weeks of the spring semester without incident. She told me that immediately following the first counseling session, the inflammatory talk and physical intimidation had stopped. Anna finished the year successfully. Perhaps the positive changes that Anna was making were helping her mother, as well, because Anna's mother had stopped picking fights with school personnel.

Discussion

John Littrell and I met in 1991 through our mutual interest in brief counseling. I was the counselor in this 1996 case, but John and I collaborated on the case's conceptualization and on the final stages of writing. As a practicing school counselor, I view John as both a mentor and a colleague and despite the distance from Alaska to Iowa, e-mail bridges the distance.

I want to emphasize that no formulaic solution was imposed on my clients. It was essential that the peripheral adults, including me, were restricted from intervening. This left my clients to evaluate themselves as they worked toward a positive outcome. Since conflict is an ongoing fact of life, each of these young women will be afforded other opportunities to use her newly acquired insights and skills. I experienced a deep satisfaction in helping them negotiate this conflict.

References

DeJong, P., & Berg, I.K. (1998). *Interviewing for solutions*. Pacific Grove, CA: Brooks/Cole.

de Shazer, S. (1988). *Clues: Investigating solutions in brief therapy*. New York: W. W. Norton.

Fisch, R., Weakland, J.H., & Segal, L. (1982). *The tactics of change: Doing therapy briefly*. San Francisco: Jossey-Bass.

Littrell, J. M. (1998). *Brief counseling in action.* New York: W. W. Norton.
Watzlawick, P., Weakland, J., & Fisch, R. (1974). *Change: Principles of problem formation and problem resolution.* New York: W. W. Norton.

Biographical Statements

Kirk Zinck, MA, is a doctoral candidate in Marriage and Family Therapy, Iowa State University. He was, at the time this was written, a high school counselor in Alaska. He is a Licensed Marriage and Family Therapist with a private practice in Seldovia, Alaska. You can reach Kirk at kzinck@iastate.edu.

John M. Littrell, EdD, is professor of counselor education at Iowa State University, Ames. He presented 25 national workshops for the American Counseling Association on the topic of brief counseling. John authored *Brief Counseling in Action* (1998) and produced five brief counseling videotapes. He is writing a research-based book about an exemplary elementary school counselor. You can reach John at jlittrel@iastate.edu.

During the past four years, John and Kirk have coauthored two articles and three book chapters, and coproduced a brief counseling videotape. Their collaboration as researchers is ongoing.

CHAPTER 13

Weathering an Adolescent Storm

Dorothy Breen

Surely there is a family somewhere that moves children easily and smoothly through adolescence. Maybe somewhere over the rainbow! Dorothy Breen describes a family that is clearly within the "functional" range. Katie, nevertheless, confronts her parents with serious behavioral problems. Communication between Katie and her parents has all but stopped. There is no history of physical or emotional problems, or substance or physical abuse. So why was Katie upset enough to threaten to run away or kill herself?

Due to limitations imposed by time, Breen limits her goals: to improve communication between mother and daughter and to secure Katie's commitment not to run away or attempt suicide. Her strategies were appropriate to a short-term intervention: reframing Katie's worrisome behaviors as normal teen rebellion and facilitating communication by encouraging positive messages and accurate listening. The goals were achieved in seven sessions spaced out over about four months.

"I wish my parents would get off my back!" Sound familiar? This is a typical cry of many adolescents who talk with me in my office. Fifteen-year-old Katie was one of them.

Mary, Katie's mother, called me when Katie threatened to run away from home and, in fact, had made one attempt to leave. Mary said: "We don't get along with our daughter. Her father and I have a hard time communicating with her and she doesn't respect us." Mary called me three weeks before I was about to go away for a month. I told her I could see them, but I thought it would be best to wait until I returned rather than to have three sessions and then break for a month. However, there was an urgency in Mary's voice. She was also concerned about Katie's failing grades in her first year of high school and she preferred to begin right away. So we did.

At the initial session, Mary told me that Katie liked to spend most of her time alone in her room listening to music or watching television. Occasionally, she visited friends at their homes but rarely invited them to visit at her own home. Communication between Katie and her parents consisted mostly of arguing about rules. Katie often felt sad and had occasional thoughts of killing herself. I confronted Katie on this and it was clear that her suicidal ideation was a "message" rather than a serious threat.

Both parents were employed full time, Mary as a radiology technician and John as a carpenter. In addition, Mary and John attended vocational school. Katie's 12-year-old brother, Mark, was in the seventh grade, a good student, and seemed to get along well with all family members.

Conceptualization

Katie was struggling with the changes that adolescents go through as they develop into independent, autonomous adults. She wanted to spend more time with her peers and less time with her family. Katie was basically a good kid and didn't get into serious trouble. She took responsibility for making her bed, washing the dishes, cleaning the bathroom, and helping with laundry. Although school was uninteresting to her, she attended every day. Katie did not do one iota more than she had to at school. She didn't participate in extracurricular activities and after school went home to watch television or listen to music in her room.

The *DSM-IV-TR* diagnosis I chose was Adjustment Disorder with Depressed Mood because of Katie's reaction to what she perceived as "tightening of the reins" by her parents. Her symptoms were withdrawal from family, threats to run away from home, thoughts about killing herself, and poor grades.

I saw this as a caring family. The parents enforced appropriate rules. For example, curfew was 9:00 in the evening during the school week, no telephone use was allowed past 9:30, no boys were permitted in the house when the parents weren't home, no boys were allowed upstairs even if the parents were home, and the kids had to be responsible for their chores. They shared a family dinner each evening and attended church together every Sunday. Grandparents, great grandparents, aunts, uncles, and cousins lived nearby and visited often. There was no history of physical or emotional problems, substance abuse, or physical abuse. So why was Katie so sad and angry? Why did she threaten to run away from home?

Mary and John resisted the changes Katie was going through. They didn't like her friends because they were afraid they would get Katie into trouble. They wanted Katie to participate in extracurricular school activities or work at a part-time job, situations where they would know what was going on. Katie refused. As Katie pushed to spend unapproved time away from home, her parents became more anxious. Behind Katie's back, they would call her friends' parents to check on her. They drove around at night looking for her. They even called the police to get them to look for her. Katie was sometimes dishonest with her parents and, unfortunately, Mary and John were not always honest with Katie. Her parents were trying to make sure she was safe and Katie interpreted their efforts as interference, pressure, and distrust.

Mary and Katie fell into a poor communication pattern. Whenever Mary asked Katie to do something she did not want to do, they ended up yelling. One very important thing was missing and that was the expression of love that I knew Mary felt for her daughter.

Arguing and worrying can push loving and caring into the background. Most parents know that it's healthy for their children to differentiate. The challenge is to foster differences, to allow teens to develop their own personalities, and still get along with them. The relationship becomes so strained that parents are unable to tell their children what they like about them.

My job was to get the family to begin talking again. Talking, not yelling. I asked Katie and her parents to attend sessions together so that they could work on communication skills. Mark did not participate in the counseling. The family thought it was not important to include him because he was not presenting problems. Ironically, I think Katie saw Mark as a problem precisely because her parents did not see him as a problem. According to Katie, Mark got away with murder. Maybe I should have included him but it was hard enough to find a time when only three members of this busy family could attend sessions and so we went forward without Mark.

Due to limitations imposed by time, mine as well as theirs, I decided to limit our goals: (1) improve communication between Mary and Katie and (2) secure Katie's commitment not to run away or attempt suicide. I decided that improving Katie's grades would be beyond the scope of counseling. The family accepted these goals. Of course, I hoped that if the argumentation between mother and daughter and the stress generated by Katie's threats were reduced, improved grades might be a secondary gain.

The strategies I used were (1) reframing Katie's worrisome behaviors as normal teen rebellion, and (2) facilitating communication by encouraging positive messages and accurate listening. Between sessions I assigned homework, including writing and talking about feelings and engaging in pleasurable activities together, such as watching movies and playing board games.

▒ Process

<u>Session 1.</u> The family sat in the three rocking chairs in my office, with Katie in the middle. Katie made it clear that she was in counseling only because her mom and dad were forcing her to be there. She had an angry look on her face and sat with her arms folded. Her mom and dad were very quiet with stern

expressions. My first impression was, "Another angry teenager. Her parents want me to fix her and don't want to examine their role."

The purpose of this initial interview was to gather information. Mary did most of the talking. I tried to get Katie involved by asking her routine questions about birth dates and address. There were some smiles when Katie did not know her parents' exact ages and I asked her to guess. These first sessions are tense, and a sense of humor is so important! Given the tense atmosphere of most initial interviews, adolescents are pleasantly surprised when I find something to laugh about. I do have to guard against using humor that embarrasses teenagers because they can be so sensitive. So, in the case of remembering birthdays, a direct question puts the individual on the spot, "Do you remember your parents' birthdays?" It's safer to ask them to guess how old they think their parents are.

Katie began to talk and smile. She told me about her school, what her parents did for work, and what she liked to do with her spare time.

I give children the first chance to tell me why they have been brought to counseling. They know that the reason is because of their misbehavior! But when I asked Katie why she and her parents were there, she said, "I don't know." Come to think of it, this is a typical response. Unfortunately, it dampened the mood. Family members were no longer smiling and the arguing began, mostly between Katie and Mary.

Mary:	(*Arms folded in front of her, jaw tightly clenched.*) Yes, you do know. You fight with us about the rules and whenever we ask you to do something you don't want to do, you argue and yell at us.
Katie:	(*Angrily.*) Well, you never let me do *anything*.

Mary used the words "us" and "we" as if she spoke for herself and John. John quietly went along with whatever Mary said. I asked Katie if she argued with her dad. She said they didn't argue because he didn't question her.

In this family, Mary played the role of "heavy." It wasn't that John wasn't at home. In fact, John was usually home from work before Mary, and he made the family meal each evening. John just didn't make any demands. Each day when Mary came home from work, she interrogated Katie about schoolwork and household chores. At least John wasn't sabotaging Mary's attempts at discipline. Whatever impact John's passivity had on the marital relationship, I maintained my focus, as had been agreed, upon communication problems between Mary and Katie.

I confronted Katie directly about her threats of running away and suicide. Such threats are often a cry to be heard. Katie confirmed that this was the case. I suggested a deal. Katie would stop her threats and, in return, her mother would listen carefully to what she had to say. Mary and Katie agreed to my deal.

In this first session, I wanted to do something helpful about the communication problem. I asked them to think about one positive thing they could say to each other. There was silence and all three squirmed in their chairs. As I expected, Mary responded first.

Mary:	Oh, I don't know, I guess one positive thing is that Katie takes responsibility for doing her chores at home.
Counselor:	Katie, did you know that your mother appreciates that you take responsibility for doing your chores?
Katie:	(*With a half smile.*) No.

I complimented Mary for making the effort to be positive, recognizing how hard it is for a parent to be positive at the same time she is angry. As we then discussed, negative communication had become a pattern.

I assigned homework: they were to give each other at least one positive statement during the week. I reminded Katie of her commitment not to run away or attempt suicide.

Session 2. They had not carried out my communications assignment. I facilitated communication between Mary and Katie. I asked Katie to repeat back what her mother said to her and Mary to repeat back what Katie said to her. Once again, John spoke only when I asked him a direct question and his responses were always in line with Mary's.

Katie said that she wanted to make more of her own decisions and have more responsibility.

| Mary: | Now Katie, we'd like to let you make your own decisions, but how can we when you just failed two courses? You never talk to us about your schoolwork. You never tell us what's going on. We found out when it was too late. |
| Katie: | (*Annoyed.*) I can't stand it when you ask me so many questions. You never stop! |

I got agreement for another homework assignment. Katie would talk to her mother more about her schoolwork and Mary would not ask so many pointed questions. Specifically, Katie would tell her mom each night about her assignments, show her what she had done, and discuss with her a plan for finishing the remaining work. Mary would acknowledge Katie's accomplishments and not ask questions. They would refrain from yelling, arguing, or "put downs."

They hesitated to accept this assignment because they didn't know when they would have time to carry it out. So we had to work on designating a time each night.

Session 3. They had worked hard over the week and felt good about completing the homework. Rather than asking Mary and Katie how the week went, I decided to ask John what he had observed. I had a hunch that he was very well aware of the dynamics between Mary and Katie but avoided putting himself in the middle.

Counselor:	John, how did Mary and Katie do with their homework assignment?
John:	I think they did OK.
Counselor:	What did you notice?

John: They took the time to sit down and talk to each other. It was nice to see. Usually they get into yelling and it just gets worse and worse. But this week they tried to be nice to each other.

Mary and Katie were obviously interested in hearing what John had to say. Smiles broke out as if their new behavior had been officially validated. John's observer role had been useful to me!

There was more sensitivity evident during this session. It is not easy for parents to just listen when their child talks about serious problems. However, Mary and John were very attentive as Katie discussed thoughts about killing herself. She didn't want to feel that way but didn't believe anyone could help. Sometimes it helped to talk to friends, but she didn't believe they really understood. Like most teenagers, Katie felt that her emotional experience was unique on the planet.

Counselor: What would happen if you talked to mom and dad about how you feel?

Katie: Are you kidding? She would drill me with more questions!

Katie wanted to tell her mom how she was feeling and have her just listen. That's all, just listen. Mary truly believed that she was being helpful by asking questions. Naturally, as a caring mother she wanted to know as much as she could about any situation.

Mary said that she would make a point of listening and hoped that Katie would tell her about her friends and would invite her friends to visit.

Katie: *(Angrily.)* They don't like my friends and they don't even know them! So why should I even bother talking about them?

I framed this as, "Katie wants to tell you about her friends but does not want you to be too quick to form judgments about them." Mary and John said they would try to refrain from judgment.

We would not meet again for a month, since I would be away. Although I truly did not believe a contract was necessary any longer, I got Katie to agree that she would neither run away or attempt suicide.

Session 4. Katie was obviously upset and didn't even say hello when she came into my office. She sat down and did not look at any of us. Naturally, I assumed that the family had had a bad month.

Thankfully, John and Mary reported that things had gone well. Katie had been telling them more about school and her friends. She had even had her boyfriend over to the house a few times. She was better than ever about doing her chores.

So why did Katie look unhappy?

John: We had a blowup in the car on the way here. Katie wants to go to Becky's house tonight for an overnight. The kids plan to get together at Becky's and then go out somewhere from there. We said she could go but we want her to call and tell us where they're going, how they're going to get there, and what time they plan to get back to Becky's house. We told her we wouldn't bombard her with lots of other questions like we used to. But we insist she tell us those things.

Katie wanted to go to Becky's and not have to call home. She feared that her parents would keep her on the phone asking lots of questions. Mary and John stuck to their guns. If she did not call with the information, the consequence would be that her parents would call Becky's parents and/or come looking for her. Katie could avoid this embarrassment by calling, herself. Katie whined, "They don't understand what it's like to be a kid," but went along with the arrangement.

<u>Session 5.</u> Mary began with a painful issue.

Mary:	I really don't like it when Katie tells me she hates me.
Counselor:	Have you told Katie how it makes you feel when she says she hates you?
Mary:	No.
Counselor:	Tell her now.
Mary:	(*Awkwardly looking at Katie.*) It hurts me when you say you hate me. (*Silence.*)
Counselor:	Katie, what do you have to say?
Katie:	I don't know.
Counselor:	Do you hate your mom?
Katie:	No.
Counselor:	Well, what do you mean when you say you hate her? Tell your mom.
Katie:	(*Awkwardly.*) I hate it when you yell at me and ask so many questions.

It was wonderful to see the anger vanish from Katie's face. Through more facilitated dialogue they moved from hate to expressions of love and respect! How can something so simple as saying "I love you" be so difficult? The nurturing, caring expression hidden inside Mary became beautifully expressed in her smile. Mary looked across toward John and there was tenderness in their glances.

At this point Katie asserted herself.

Katie:	I do a lot of positive things and I would like it if mom and dad acknowledged those instead of just telling me when I do things wrong.
Counselor:	Katie, can you give your mom and dad an example of what you were thinking about?
Katie:	Yeah. Like when I called home Saturday night to let you know where I was.
John:	We do appreciate that and I guess we could have said "thanks for calling," huh?
Katie:	Yeah.

Counselor:	Katie, was there something positive *you* could have said to your parents at that time, too?
Katie:	Yeah, I guess I could have thanked them for not asking me a ton of questions.

Session 6. Katie reported that they got along well during the past two weeks. I pointed out that I saw less tension and resentment when they talked with each other. Katie said her mom and dad were giving her more positive messages and Mary and John said that Katie was less antagonistic. So, we discussed how they could spend more time together, given outside commitments. Both Katie and Mary liked to play board games and they decided to do that. John and Katie would cook dinner together. They would all go for walks.

Katie reported that she no longer felt like she wanted to run away from home. The family would take a break from counseling and return in six weeks for a follow-up.

Outcome

Session 7. Katie, once again, did not say anything as she entered my office, took her seat, and sulked. Mary and John smiled, did not seem concerned about Katie, and said things were going very well. How could this be?

Counselor:	Katie, I can't help but notice that your posture and expression are not consistent with what your mother and father are telling me.
Katie:	(*Looking up suddenly.*) I'm okay. We just came here from the orthodontist and I found out that I couldn't have my braces off today. He told me he would take them off this time and now he tells me I have to wait another month!
Mary:	It's real disappointing for her.
John:	You've done real well with your braces and you really wanted them off.

Katie sat up straight and stopped sulking. Her parents had validated her feelings and the negative pattern of communication had been reversed. The more Katie talked to her parents, the less need they felt to interrogate her; the fewer pointed questions they asked, the more comfortable Katie was sharing information.

Discussion

I believe that the keys to rapid progress in this case were (1) the decision to include Mary and John rather than treating Katie individually, (2) the decision to stick to attainable goals, and (3) the fact that this was basically a healthy family to start with.

It was not difficult for me to identify with the problems this family brought to counseling. As a single parent I struggled with the innumerable responsibilities of parenting and working. I was usually consumed with that and exhausted. I had to remind myself constantly that my priority was my daughter. I was responsible for raising a healthy, happy daughter. I set aside time to be available to listen and to talk with her and to spend time having fun with her. It was not always enjoyable spending time with a kid who was going through continuing emotional ups and downs and who challenged me as she gained her independence. However, it was worthwhile.

During the follow-up session, John said: "We may still have some flare-ups to face, but I believe we now have the tools we need to take care of things." John had perfectly expressed my own hopes and expectations for his family.

Reference

American Psychiatric Association. (2000). *Diagnostic and statistical manual of mental disorders: DSM-IV-TR* (4th ed., text revision). Washington, DC: Author.

Biographical Statement

Dorothy Breen, PhD, is associate professor of Counselor Education at the University of Maine. Her writing and research interests focus on changing family structures; relationships between students, teachers, and parents; and using play techniques with children and adolescents in schools. Her published articles include "Moral Dilemmas of Early Adolescents of Divorced and Intact Families," which appeared in the *Journal of Early Adolescence* (1993). She serves on the editorial board of the *Journal of Research in Rural Education*. Dorothy is also a licensed psychologist and has a part-time private practice with children and adolescents. You can reach Dorothy at dorothy_breen@voyager.umeres.maine.edu.

CHAPTER 14

Where Do I Fit?

Marijane Fall

Marijane Fall's case study presents a parent's nightmare: Joe, a previously well-behaved teenager, is experimenting with drugs, getting D's and F's, and showing signs of a serious depression. A creeping "nothingness" is consuming Joe's life. The counseling goes beautifully and in five sessions Joe straightens himself out. Why did this case go forward smoothly to a successful outcome? Fall worries about whether the celebration was premature. Four months later, Joe and his family call with the good news that the gains are ongoing.

It's not easy to figure out why counseling sometimes fails and at other times succeeds. In this case, there seems to be a perfect match between Fall's deeply held Adlerian philosophy and a goal-oriented teen client with high cognitive ability. If you, the reader, are a fan of Alfred Adler, you will love this case.

He walked in dressed in uniform, with pants hanging on his hip bones and falling down over his sneakers, flannel shirt large and loose over a black tee shirt, black hair falling over his face on one side, and a sullen look on his face. Joe, 15, followed behind his parents, appearing to wait with guarded arrogance for them to tell him what to do. His eyes were mainly cast down, though he looked up when I spoke. He was a handsome young man, tall, slightly overweight, as if his weight hadn't yet distributed over his tall, big-boned frame.

Joe's parents, John and Ann, called me on a referral from a friend. Although my practice as a therapist encompassed young children, teens, and adults, in actuality I worked mainly with teens. The parents were concerned about (a) Joe's change in grades from all A's and B's to C's, D's, and an F, (b) his lack of interest in the family and seclusion in his room at home, (c) a change for the worse in his friends, and (d) his apparent depression and increased sleeping. Joe was worried, too, and agreed to try therapy. He told me about school and a lack of connectedness with peers. Last year he had been very much a part of the social scene at school and on weekends. This year he felt left out of two main groups in the school—the "druggies," whom Joe saw as "fun but way out at times," and the "preppies," who were "immature." Second, Joe complained of a "nothingness" that was with him most of the time. He wanted to go to college but was unable to motivate himself to study. Two weeks ago he had told his parents, "Maybe I don't study because I never had to work for grades. Now, if I work, I might fail." Whew! Insight already and we had hardly gotten started!

Our first meeting consisted of (a) time with Joe, John, and Ann, (b) time alone with John and Ann, (c) time alone with Joe, and (d) a concluding brief meeting of us all. At our joint opening time, I explained confidentiality guidelines: I wouldn't share what Joe and I talked about unless he gave me permission, was a danger to self or others, or I was ordered to do so by the courts. I explained my point of view about counseling with teens: Joe knows what his problems are better than I do and so my role is to be a catalyst. By mutual agreement, we went over the client intake forms together so that all family members would know what the others' perceptions of the difficulties were. Finally, we set another appointment in a few weeks.

As the parents detailed their concerns with me, I was aware of interesting family dynamics. John was angry because Joe had stopped trying in sports and lost his position on the team. He wasn't studying. Perhaps the worst part was that no matter how John tried, Joe would not communicate with him in words, answering questions with monosyllables. Ann's concerns were about Joe's negative attitude, his failing grades, his time alone in his room, and his change in friends. Joe no longer spent time with his former friends, nice young people whom his parents liked. John and Ann appeared to like each other and valued family above all else. I listened, reflected, validated them for not giving up and for bringing Joe here, and reiterated how hard it was to be a parent.

When Joe entered the room for his private time with me, he was mad! He had felt left out of the discussion when I met with his parents. "I just want you to know that I don't like that. Don't treat me like that!" Although this was not what I expected, I was impressed with his power and wondered if he could make it work for him.

Joe's conversation centered around the social scene at high school. He had been a class leader throughout middle school and somewhat of a leader in ninth grade as well. Now, he could not find his position of leadership or importance and no one seemed to notice him anymore. "Others would tell me that I'm a leader. I'd tell them that I am just a good actor." He regarded his former friends as dull, immature, and boring. New friends were "big time druggies," using acid a lot. He admitted to worries about substance use although he claimed to have used no more than a few times.

My time with Joe was short, only 40 minutes. Yet, beginning with his anger, I felt that we had talked of important things. I had ruled out suicidal behavior ("I thought about it, but I'm not willing to give up my life plans for that!"), and I had begun to fill in some parts of a picture of Joe. He would go to school, smoke a joint before school, go to class, (maybe smoke more?), go home, go to his room to sleep, eat, and go to his room and go to bed for the night. When asked to show how much time each week was "sad," "nothingness," and "relatively happy" (his terms), Joe graphed approximately 30 percent of a circle as sad, 10 percent as relatively happy, and 60 percent as nothingness.

I listened reflectively to Joe. I attempted to reflect his choices, to point out his power, and to validate him. I also used VERY tentative language in my reflections ("It sounds like ..., I wonder if ..., Does that mean you were feeling? ... ").

Conceptualization

I seldom find diagnosis via *DSM* codes to be clear and accurate after a first visit. Joe presented symptoms of Major Depressive Disorder (*DSM-IV*). However, I had questions concerning his use of drugs. Was a substance etiologically related to the mood disturbance? If so, then the diagnosis of Unknown Substance-Induced Mood Disorder would prevail. Since Joe's parents chose to pay for therapy rather than have to adhere to their medical health insurance guidelines, I was not forced into an early exact diagnosis. A recent medical checkup lessened concerns about a physical basis for changes in Joe. I also decided against referring him for antidepressants pending further investigation due to his present use of illegal substances. The last thing a substance-abusing teen needs is a psychoactive drug that can be used inappropriately. In retrospect, though to this day I am still not sure, I suspect that substances played a large part in Joe's depressed mood.

I wrote down goals as I heard them from Joe. These would be discussed again at the second session, corrected as needed, and used to work from in subsequent sessions. The goals were worded very tentatively because I could see that it was so important for Joe to be in control:

1. It sounds like you want to control the nothingness instead of vice versa, and you would like us to work on that.
2. You want to find some friends more similar to you. Are you also wondering about the kind of person you want to be with friends?
3. Is a third goal that you want your parents to continue listening to you as they have just started doing?

Although Joe confirmed that all of the goals were desirable, he proceeded to focus on the need for friends and belongingness. Since it is my belief that depression is helped by taking small successful steps, I suggested that Joe have some form of sustained physical exercise for half an hour every other day. The exercise could help reduce his weight, although it was a minor concern, and could also combat depression. Joe agreed to walk and jog, though he refused to commit to how often he would.

I have strong Adlerian leanings. The first stage of Adlerian therapy is to establish a relationship of nonjudgmental acceptance and empathy. Adlerian philosophy's tentative language of hypotheses (i.e., "could it be ..., I'm wondering if ...") fits well with the defensive position of most teens toward adult authority. Thus, I work from the client's goals, using the counseling relationship to establish a safe place, and using reflection of meaning and feelings to allow the client to explore situations. Surprisingly, Joe asked me for information about the effects of drugs. This educational component also fit well within the Adlerian framework. I used the Adlerian view of social needs and the need for importance to assist in the formation of hypotheses concerning Joe's life-style. I formed my hypotheses as a result of an analysis of how Joe needed to function in the world and what seemed to be missing in his current functioning.

Process

By way of an overview, I met Joe for five sessions on December 6 and 13, and January 2, 9, and 20. The dates are important, since school was not in session in late December and during that time Joe's family went away for a skiing vacation. The interruption from daily interaction with peers and increased family time provided an opportunity to work on family relationships. Following is information from these individual sessions and an explanation of how they related to our individual goals.

Joe set the agenda for our second session on his need to be connected to friends. As Joe talked, I handed him some pieces of clay I labeled "Mom," "Dad," "Bob" (older brother away at college), and "Joe." I asked him to mold these hunks of clay in a sort of "pictorama" and show how they all related. He placed the Mom and Dad fairly close together with Mom in the middle between Joe and Dad. Bob was placed far away from everyone. He went on to tell of conflicts with Dad over sports and grades. "He never talks to me, just says, do this, do that." Joe said that he knew his parents loved him, and he liked when the family went away on trips or did things together.

A second clay pictorama of Joe with his peers opened dialog about his confusion and ambivalence. He wanted to continue to be an integral part of a group of kids, "to be a leader and at the center of them," but he didn't like the choices anymore. In one group he perceived that he needed to do drugs and have frequent sex to belong. In the other group he felt that members "just talk stupid about nothing."

I was very much interested in the next development. Joe talked about drugs currently in use by the "druggies." He asked about the characteristics of these drugs, if they were addictive, and what the long-term effects were. I relayed information I knew and said I'd gather more for our next meeting. He spoke of more involvement with drugs than at the intake, after being assured that I would not tell his parents unless his life was in danger. Smoking pot before, during, and after school was his typical pattern, with acid being used on weekends and at parties. Some students had cocaine. Joe's questions revolved around just how much he could take before it affected him in some way. Although we talked in a fairly abstract way about this, I sensed that Joe was weighing the facts very carefully. I was surprised that he didn't try to debate with me.

Joe's insight into his behaviors was promising. For example, he mentioned that studies, sports, and leadership came easily. He didn't have to work very hard to be "the best" in years past. However, now others were really trying and were beating him. "If I don't try and I fail, I can blame it on that, but if I really work and they beat me, it will be my fault." Joe's high expectations for himself were working against him.

I experienced a level of rapport with Joe that had not been present at our first meeting. I also sensed his growing trust that this was a safe place. He had felt unable to speak to either peers or parents about his concerns as his peers began to use more and more drugs. Our dialog was easy as we moved clay "people" around to illustrate Joe's perception of reality or to explore possibilities.

John and Ann met with me on the week following Joe's second visit. Joe and I had discussed what I could share with them. He did not want information concerning drug use to be shared but gave permission to communicate anything else that would be helpful. He was comfortable with my consultation with his parents, in contrast to the first visit, when he had reacted so strongly against it. I suspect that he understood that I would be working to help things improve in his relationship with his parents.

John and Ann had their own twofold agenda. They needed to share their fears and wished for help in communicating better with Joe. John took the lead, telling me all that was wrong and allowing me little interaction with Ann. However, she spoke up eventually and suggested that he didn't listen, a behavior that irritated Joe. John acknowledged this, and we were off on an educational path. I suggested readings that taught simple listening skills such as tracking and reflection. After I demonstrated skills, they practiced and laughed at themselves struggling with the right words. They were eager learners and gave each other constructive feedback. I invited them to call if they felt the need for another separate meeting with me.

Two weeks passed between my second and third meeting with Joe. He had been out of school and told me that the vacation with his parents had been fun. He felt closer to them and said that communication was improved. He was anxious to talk about his peer relationships again, but first mentioned that he had been studying and had started to improve his grades. He said that he cared about his academics for the first time. He appeared pleased, and I reflected that he had taken charge of his studies for his own reasons, not someone else's.

Confusion about right or wrong, good and bad was the central theme of this third visit.

- Drugs are not good but they feel great.
- I am afraid to abuse chemicals but others do it and they get by.
- I'm intelligent and this stupid boy gets the girl I want.
- I treat girls with respect and not as sex objects but I don't have a girlfriend.
- I want good grades and I don't want to do homework.

Joe said he had been thinking of all these things over and over, "It's like it used to work, but the same formula doesn't work anymore."

I felt the same ease and trust between us as I had the previous session. Joe was moving, feeling much less of the nothingness that had been his presenting concern.

He felt connected to parents and was making new decisions about schoolwork. He reported that he was not going to use drugs during the week and was thinking about a change on weekends as well. Despite the confusion, he was taking charge of his life.

Session four brought further surprises. Joe said he was happy most of the time and was trying on a new "non-grunge" look at school. "My friends asked about the look and I told them I was making new choices now." Joe also said he was trying out new friends and was thinking that he might form his own group, closer to the "immature" group than the "druggies." He felt he could still be friendly with everyone, but be special friends with just these few. Other new decisions were to study more and to decide for himself what is safe as far as chemical substances.

We talked about what else we needed to do and future meetings. It was decided to meet one more time, with the possibility that it would be our last session unless a need arose. Joe's strength was much in evidence. He was getting along well at home, had eliminated the depressing nothingness, and was finding a place at school. Change was happening, and Joe felt his personal power in bringing this about.

Our fifth session was our last. We talked of where Joe had been two months ago, where he now was, and where he wished to be in the future. He said he hoped to continue feeling as good as he now did, but he knew he could handle it if he didn't. Since Joe had reduced his drug use greatly, I asked how much influence over his mood he attributed to drugs. He said he couldn't tell, but that he had only started using fairly heavily in October and November as he experimented with the "druggie" peer group.

This last session left me feeling a bit disconnected. I had felt strongly connected to Joe in the second session, but less intensely so in the third, fourth, and fifth sessions. Although there was a good working relationship between us, Joe came and went quickly from my appointment book. Was his changed attitude only temporary? Did he really progress as fast as he had seemed to? If so, how come? Had I made a mistake in my belief that he was ready to stop?

Outcome

Four months later a telephone call from John brought the news I needed to hear! Joe made honor roll for two quarters in a row, was playing for the varsity baseball team, was actively preparing for the college selection process, participated in the family, and best of all, was usually happy. Joe got on the phone and said that previous concerns were no longer his choices (I assume he meant drug use since he disguised the content of his words). He reported that the "nothingness" had been banished. Joe's dad got back on the phone and heaped praise on me for giving him back his son. I had to acknowledge that I was only a catalyst. Joe was the one with the courage and power to get through this developmental crisis. There were others deserving of praise, primarily John and Ann, who had been astute, noticed changes, and had sought help early when usual interventions didn't help. They had worked hard to improve their listening skills and were raising a strong young man with good ego strength and clearly developed insight.

Discussion

So what really happened in those five sessions with Joe? How was he able to move himself from such a stuck place to one of such productivity? I will share the results of my meandering and let you, the reader, decide. I think that John and Ann started the road to recovery when they insisted that things were not OK and tried to really hear what Joe was saying. Joe said that there was a change starting when the appointment with me was made. "For the first time they accepted that this was really bad for me," said Joe. Thus, Joe no longer had to escalate risky behaviors in order to get the attention he sought. His cry for help was heard.

Most adolescents are not ready for personal change when they come to counseling, only for the change of others. Joe was an exception. He hated the experience he called "nothingness" that I think was his brain's reaction to the chemical substances he was using. He was clear on what he wanted in terms of leadership, friends, and the future. I suspect that he was already beginning to worry about his use of drugs, yet could think of no place to seek the information that he desired. Joe did not want to be drugged out and burned out like some of his friends were in the fall of the year. He held on to a different picture of himself as a strong leader. All these attributes in Joe and in his parents' approach to the situation were in his favor.

I still ponder the relationship between us. We had not had the immediate rapport that I am most used to in working with children and adolescents. For example, I always tell clients that at the end of the first session we will discuss whether this is a good match to work together and if not, then I'll help them find a therapist who fits better. I usually feel that clients will want to come back to me but with Joe I was not sure. Another odd thing was that the intimacy had been strongest during the second session and then became less intense. With adolescents I walk the line between intimacy and separation, between success and failure, and between the conditions of nonjudgmental positive regard and disdain. With Joe, I felt my way very slowly and carefully. I think that my recognition of his power during that very first interview is part of the difference in the intimacy/separation tightrope. Joe was strong. He had been able to tell me his feelings immediately ("Don't treat me like that again."). I wanted to see him take charge of his distressing situation as well, and he needed to feel his own power in doing this. Although the need for adolescents to connect is strong, developmentally the need to separate may be even stronger. For these reasons, I may have held back more than I might with a weak individual.

I want to call attention to some creative techniques that really helped. The clay pieces illustrated Joe's social situations and were a medium of communication. When he graphed the nothingness in relation to sadness and happiness, I had a reference point for change. A third technique that worked well for Joe was to take an emotional temperature reading of the preceding week. This allowed me to reflect how Joe was taking charge of change, so necessary for his self-image as a leader. These techniques helped with the "intensity border," which can be especially troublesome for adolescent clients. The focus can be on the technique for a time, then switch back to the person. This change can allow much-needed space for teens who are in the uncomfortable throes of separation from family at the same time that they need family.

As a counselor, I am left with issues for my growth. I'm never exactly sure why some relationships work so well and others less well. Brief therapy gives me even less time to evaluate the progress and outcomes. Perhaps this is why I am so excited about and energized by my work. It is always in process, as is my growth as a therapist.

Reference

American Psychiatric Association. (2000). *Diagnostic and statistical manual of mental disorders: DSM-IV-TR* (4th ed., text revision). Washington, DC: Author.

Biographical Statement

Marijane Fall, EdD, is associate professor at the University of Southern Maine. She has a small private practice in which she specializes in counseling children and adolescents and supervising others with similar practices. Marijane is a registered play therapist and supervisor and a licensed counselor in Maine. Her research focuses on counseling interventions with children in schools. You can reach Marijane at mjfall@usm.maine.edu.

CHAPTER 15

Oh, Give Me a Home

Scottie Sue Landess and Nola Christenberry

Scottie Sue Landess provides supportive counseling for an abused teen. She collaborates with agency personnel and encourages her client to use the court system to meet his needs. Today's school counselors will identify with Landess's frustration as she confronts irresponsible parents and guardians, as well as legal obstacles to working with abused and neglected youngsters.

At the time of this case, Jerry was nearly 16 years old and in the ninth grade. He was the oldest of five children, the others being Sam, 13, Patty, 12, Susan, 9, and Leon, 8. At age 10, Patty had been removed from the home by her maternal grandmother without parental opposition.

I first met Jerry on the playground when he was in second grade. During the years since, he told me about washing his face with dirty underwear and picking roaches out of his cereal, which he ate with water instead of milk. He told me of being the primary caretaker for his younger siblings because of his parents' alcohol abuse and their involvement in producing, selling, and using illegal drugs. The Division of Family Services (DFS) had been "on their case" for at least nine years.

I was the only counselor for 500 students in the K-12 rural school that Jerry and his siblings attended, and I worked with all of them in classroom guidance activities. All buildings are on one campus that is bounded by farmland. For all practical purposes, the school is the town.

The school population is 98% Caucasian, with the other 2% being primarily migrant students of Hispanic origin. Like I did, many of the teachers in the school have K-12 assignments and are, therefore, quite familiar with the students and their families. Yet, most of them were reluctant to become involved with Jerry and his family. These teachers expected students to be ready to learn and were unwilling to take the home situation into account.

My contact with Jerry increased during ninth grade. Early in the year, he asked for help with failing grades. After that, he would stop me in the hallway or come by my office with requests for small items such as pencils. Then he came to me with the story that ultimately would change his life (see Session 3).

Dr. Nola Christenberry was and still is my professor and advisor and friend. She helped me process my thoughts about Jerry and assisted in writing this case.

Conceptualization

Several *DSM-IV-TR* labels could fit Jerry, but I don't think that assignment of labels is particularly useful in the school setting. As a consequence of neglect and abuse in the home, Jerry had social and academic difficulties at school that worsened each year.

As Jerry's parents were sinking further into the drug scene, Jerry felt he was being forced to become responsible for the upbringing and care of his siblings. He was the "chief cook and bottle washer." He was in charge of laundry, and there was no washer or dryer. In fact, there was no stove or refrigerator, no heat or hot water. Jerry did laundry at the home of a neighbor when she wasn't "mad at my mother." This role of father for younger siblings under third-world conditions was wearing him down.

Jerry believed that other students were making fun of him because of his family, because he didn't bathe regularly, and because he didn't have socks to wear. So instead of playing basketball at noon, he often stopped by to chat with me, probably to avoid the humiliation of not having socks.

Academically, I believed that Jerry had ability to succeed in the college-prep track he had chosen. He was an A and B student throughout elementary school, but the demands of caring for younger siblings had begun to take its toll. He stopped doing the more demanding homework assignments of junior high, and his grades fell. Dreams of playing varsity basketball were dashed. Of course he was depressed; he used the word "hopeless" often.

Jerry's physical appearance led me and the school nurse to believe he was malnourished. His skin color was sallow, his hair dull, and his eyes sunken. He was extremely thin. I am unaware of any other medical conditions affecting Jerry's functioning.

My goals and strategies in working with Jerry changed over the course of his ninth-grade year. He initially sought guidance with homework, coping with rules of new teachers, and getting tutoring for his younger brother Sam, who was repeating the seventh grade. As Jerry's confidence in me increased, we moved from dealing with school issues to dealing with issues of neglect and abuse.

My goal was to empower Jerry to get himself and his siblings out of their adverse living conditions. A secondary goal was to help him do well in school. I scheduled sessions so that Jerry missed a different class each time we met. Time before and after school was unavailable because of his child-care responsibilities.

A solution-focused approach was my standard in working with Jerry because that's what he needed: solutions. Each time he came to me, no matter for how brief a session, he wanted a solution or at least a direction in which to look for a solution. This approach capitalizes on the power of positive thinking, and Jerry needed plenty of that!

Process

In this section, I will describe four of the longer and more significant sessions that occurred during Jerry's ninth-grade year. Keep in mind that other, often brief, contacts occurred between these sessions.

Session 1. During the third week of the school year, Jerry clomped into my office, plopped his enormous backpack on the floor, and said, "I can't keep this up." I asked, "How can I help you, Jerry?" He said that he was spending so much time helping his younger siblings with homework that he could not get his own done and was "already racking up F's." After about 30 minutes of discussion, we decided that getting tutoring before or after school was not possible, but finding a quiet place to work during lunch break was an option. We agreed that he could use space in the guidance classroom adjoining my office. This solution satisfied Jerry, but only temporarily.

Session 2. The weather grew cooler, and the gymnasium was opened for "free play" at noon. I knew that Jerry delighted in playing basketball during this social time. I noticed him on the sidelines for two or three days in a row, so I asked about his lack of participation.

Counselor:	Hey, Jerry. What's up? Did you beat the other guys so bad there's no competition for you anymore?
Jerry:	(*head hanging*) Naw.
Counselor:	Well, is there a problem we can fix?
Jerry:	I dunno.

A couple of hours passed, and Jerry came to my office ready to talk.

Jerry:	Do you still wanna know why I'm not playing ball during lunch?
Counselor:	I'm curious.
Jerry:	Well, I ain't got no socks. I mean, I got socks, it's just that Momma won't let me wear them. She says we've got to use them for wash rags and Sam and Leon needs socks worse than I do. And I say, Momma I got to have socks to play ball with my friends. She don't care. That's all she ever says about it is "I don't care."
Counselor:	Sounds like you're really mad at your Mom. And you really miss playing ball with your friends. What if I found some more socks for you? Would that help?
Jerry:	I doubt it. She'd just let Leon and Sam wear them.
Counselor:	What if you had some socks you could keep in your locker?

Jerry:	(*brightening somewhat*) Yeah, I guess. I'd have to be careful though and not let Leon or Sam see them. They'd tell, and Momma would have a fit. But, if you got socks, I'd like to try it. My feet get awful sore on the bottoms when I don't wear socks.

Between Sessions. Jerry was successful at keeping the secret and, once again, could spend time with his friends playing ball. On the other hand, now his time for studying was being sacrificed for basketball and his grades suffered. He came to me a few more times during the five minutes between classes for quick tips with homework and just to chat. Often, he would mention that he needed a pencil, some paper, a folder, a bandage, and the like. Each time Jerry made a request, I met it. A couple of times during this period, I scheduled sessions with Jerry. He would sit quietly for as many as 20 minutes before talking.

Session 3. One cold, mid-autumn morning, Jerry, in an extremely agitated state, came to my office as soon as the first bell rang. This was the interview that would change his life. Jerry paced the floor and talked nonstop for almost two hours. His emotions ran the gamut from extreme hurt to anger. He talked in detail about his home life.

Jerry:	I can't take it no more. They don't care if we eat or sleep or have clean clothes or nothing. It ain't fair that I have to do all the taking care of me and Leon and Sam and Susan while they're laying around drunk or doped up. Last night, the cops came and searched the house for this friend of theirs. He was there, but they didn't find him. I wish I had told them where he was hiding.
Counselor:	They didn't ask you?
Jerry:	Naw. They didn't know we were there. Momma and Daddy had locked us up in our room, and we knew better than to make any noise.
Counselor:	What do you mean by locked up?
Jerry:	I mean we was locked in. There's these padlocks on the outside of our bedroom door.
Counselor:	But what if the house ever caught fire?
Jerry:	We only got screens on our windows and we could just kick them out.
Counselor:	What do you mean, screens? You have glass in your windows, don't you?
Jerry:	Nope.
Counselor:	But, Jerry, the temperature was below freezing last night.
Jerry:	We ain't even got no beds to sleep on. We just got mattresses on the floor. Last night the mice even got cold. They was trying to get in bed with us. I ain't putting up with it no more. All you've heard is part of what happened last night, and last night wasn't no different than most nights.

Counselor:	Do you have a plan?
Jerry:	I know what I gotta do.
Counselor:	What's your plan?
Jerry:	I know I got to call and turn them in. You could do it for me but I want to do it.
Counselor:	What do you think will happen?
Jerry:	Somebody will come and talk to me and the kids, here at school I hope, because I ain't going back there. I know it'll make Momma mad, but she'll just have to get mad. I think she loves me but she sure don't know how to take care of us. All she really cares about is her drugs and her dealers.
Counselor:	I agree that you don't have to live like that, and I believe what you're telling me is true. If you're serious about making the hotline call yourself, you'll need to tell them what you've told me. Is that what you want?
Jerry:	(*more pensive and relaxed*) You got the number?
Counselor:	I do. Do you want to tell Sam or Leon or Susan about what you're doing?
Jerry:	No. They'd probably try to talk me out of it. Can I call from here?
Counselor:	Would you like me to leave the room while you make the call?
Jerry:	Are you kidding? I want you right here.

Jerry called DFS, and a social worker arrived at the school within an hour—a quick response. But just before the social worker arrived, Jerry's brother, Sam, stopped by, something he rarely did on his own. He shut the door and essentially repeated Jerry's story. Sam also was ready for something to be done. I brought Jerry back, and the boys agreed to meet the social worker together.

Following the meeting, the DFS social worker called for a police escort. Jerry warned the DFS worker that his parents used a scanner to monitor police activity and so had advance notice when DFS workers were coming to the home. Finding only the father at home, the social worker informed him that his children were being removed, and she collected their belongings. At Jerry's suggestion, she called his aunt who agreed to take all of the children into her home temporarily. Her home was in the same school district.

While in the aunt's home, Jerry and his siblings came to school clean and well-groomed, apparently well-fed, and with their homework done. Sam stopped sucking his thumb. The parents had no contact and were required to participate in drug rehabilitation.

The story does not end. Three months into the temporary custody arrangement, the parents wanted to regain custody. They had received counseling and parenting classes in conjunction with drug rehabilitation. They got their day in court. Jerry alone was sent back to live with them while the others remained in the homes of their aunt and grandmother. Needless to say, I was confused and upset and the DFS workers had similar reactions.

<u>Session 4.</u> Jerry did not return to school the day after he was put back in his parents' custody. I was worried. He returned the next day and came directly to my office. His arm was in a cast but he refused to tell me what happened. He said that he wanted to go to another school where his family wasn't known. He declared that he would not go home until he got help with this. He was angry with the judge who had sent him home with his parents, "I ain't gonna be his laboratory rat."

I called the DFS hotline and the sheriff's office and was fortunate to reach a deputy who came to the school. He used some influence with the judge to facilitate a court order removing Jerry from his parents. Subsequently, Jerry was placed in a foster home, several miles and several counties away. He went willingly.

Outcome

About one and one-half months passed before I saw Jerry again. The occasion was a final court date to determine permanent custody of all children in this family. Jerry arrived with his guardians, dressed well, and with a smile, which I have rarely seen. He talked to me about school, friends, and an intramural basketball team. He was happier than I had ever seen him. He asked about his siblings and his parents.

While the court requested that I attend, my input was minimal. I did testify, but not about Jerry. I was questioned about the youngest child and the procedures for being evaluated for Special Education. No questions were asked of me concerning placement.

At the end of this trying day, Jerry's siblings, including the sister who had lived with their grandmother for two years, were returned to their parents' custody. Jerry would stay with his new family, a permanent placement decision, despite much pleading by his mother. Her pleas were addressed to Jerry as well as the judge. Jerry told his mother that he had to do what was best for him. He stated that he now had friends, was active in school activities, was making good grades, and had arranged for an after-school job.

I observed the interactions between Jerry and his mother, and I never saw her really listening. I was pleased that Jerry had the courage to act in his own interest.

Discussion

This case still tugs at my heartstrings and makes me keenly aware of the comforts I take for granted. It also serves as a good example of what can be accomplished when school counselors and agency workers collaborate.

Was this case a success? I think so, and my mentor, Dr. Nola Christenberry, agrees. Of course, questions remain as to the long-term outcomes, but at least all family members received some form of supportive assistance. We attribute the unusually rapid and effective response from DFS to the fact that Jerry himself made the call and stated his needs and circumstances. DFS continues to provide family counseling three times per week for the parents and the children living in their home. DFS also provides assistance with financial management, and the mother is required to undergo unscheduled drug testing every three weeks. Sam, Patty, Leon, and Susan's school attendance is regular, their physical health appears good, and they usually have their homework done. Their grooming is deteriorating, but it is considerably better than before they were removed from the home. Leon's behavior problems at school are increasing. I am concerned that Patty is being placed in Jerry's caretaker role, but she won't talk about it. I am distrustful of the mother.

We have rarely seen children who are assertive enough to make that vital phone call. That initiative bodes well for Jerry. He talks often about joining the Air Force after graduation.

We think that the weekly classroom guidance lessons Jerry had in elementary school helped him to see the school counselor as a source of help. Subsequently, Jerry's visits to ask for pencils was his way of testing the counseling waters. Once he knew that I would help with small things, he trusted me literally with his life. We urge school counselors to pay attention to their brief and seemingly trivial interactions with students.

Reference

American Psychiatric Association. (2000). *Diagnostic and statistical manual of mental disorders: DSM-IV-TR* (4th ed., text revision). Washington, DC: Author.

Biographical Statements

Scottie Sue Landess, MSE, is the kindergarten counselor in Kennett School District in Missouri. She holds a master's degree in elementary school administration and holds K-12 school counselor certification. She is completing an EdS degree in psychology and counseling at Arkansas State University. At the time of this case, Scottie had been a school counselor for six years. You can reach Scottie at tripod@sheltonlink.com.

Nola J. Christenberry, PhD, is associate professor and coordinator of the school counselor training program at Arkansas State University. She worked in public schools as a teacher, federal programs coordinator, and Upward Bound counselor. As a counselor educator, she supervises school practicum students and interns. Nola has published articles about school-based interventions with victims of sexual abuse and school policies for responding to death. You can reach Nola at nchriste@kiowa.astate.edu.

CHAPTER 16

Raising Martin

Patrick O'Malley

With a total of 155 sessions over a seven-year period, as O'Malley himself admits, this case doesn't win a place in the Brief Therapy Hall of Fame. Consider that O'Malley is treating a youngster who has lost a father to suicide and suffers separation anxiety in relation to the surviving parent. Throw in some major oppositionality. If the essence of the brief approach is to do no more therapy than necessary, O'Malley is probably justified in regarding his work as brief or, at least, time-efficient. Further, most of the sessions were only 30 minutes long.

A child may not be emotionally ready to experience and express grief. By building a warm and trusting relationship with Martin the child, O'Malley is there when Martin the adolescent is ready to open up. O'Malley's approach is person-centered from the start. He uses solution-focused interventions to keep Martin's home and school behavior on track.

Martin benefits from O'Malley's personal experience with loss and years of counseling others who are struggling with bereavement. From a psychodynamic perspective, O'Malley fashions his role relative to his client as that of an uncle rather than a father. O'Malley predicts that Martin (like all of us) will revisit his grief experience at every stage of development.

My partner had tears in her eyes when she stopped me in the hall of our offices. She had just finished talking on the phone with a client. The client had been informed by out-of-state officials that her husband had been found dead. Suicide notes had been left for her and other family members. Although he had been missing for several days, she was shocked when the phone call came.

In that call to my partner, the client expressed fear for her 9-year-old son. She asked for a referral to a counselor who had experience working with grieving children.

I have been in practice since 1979. I am known in our community as a specialist in grief counseling. Like many practitioners, I developed an area of specialty that had personal relevance for me. Shortly after I began practice I experienced the death of my son and my father within a two-year period. As I experienced the feelings from these losses, I became aware of how little I had learned about the dynamics of grief in my academic training. I read about models of grief and developmental stages of bereavement. Theoretical models provided only a broad frame in which to understand these unique personal stories. I began listening at a deeper level to the stories of loss that were told to me.

Although I devote a great amount of my clinical time to helping families manage their lives after the death of a family member, I do not believe the therapy room is where a family should have to come to heal from their loss. Grieving should be done in the social, spiritual, and emotional community in which the family lives rather than in the clinician's office. In our culture, as families struggle through their pain, they typically are abandoned quickly by their community. The therapist's office offers a safe place in which to express and experience grief when the community's support diminishes.

Martin was brought to see me when he was 9 years old. He was the only son of Emily and Robert, who had been separated at the time of Robert's death. Emily had a daughter by a previous marriage who had married and left home. Robert was an alcoholic. He was also diagnosed with bipolar disorder but was never treated for this condition.

Martin had not received any counseling before seeing me, but did attend Alateen on a regular basis.

I saw Martin in my office for the first time in the spring of 1989. As he sat curled in a ball, his head buried in his arms, I could not imagine how we would last through the hour. I certainly did not picture having a counseling relationship with him seven years later.

Conceptualization

Martin was a complex child before his father's suicide, with a history of mood swings and angry tirades. He both loved and feared his father. Home was chaotic due to his father's alcoholism and untreated bipolar disorder. His dad could be his buddy or could disappear for days after an outburst of rage. Martin witnessed verbal and physical abuse toward his mother. His symptoms worsened after his father's death.

Family history provided one component of the information needed to conceptualize Martin's diagnosis and treatment plan. His developmental level was an additional piece of information needed to plan the treatment. Much like the stages of cognitive development, children pass through stages of grief in a developmental sequence. Children at Martin's age typically understand the permanency of death but are not sufficiently emotionally developed to express their pain directly. These children act out or internalize their feelings of loss. Consequently, when I counsel grieving children who are in the prepubescent stage of development, I attempt to maintain a relationship with them through their adolescent years. I try to see grieving children frequently enough to keep a good level of rapport so I will be in position to help them in their teenage years, when they have the capacity to express their pain more directly.

Martin's mother was more than willing for my relationship with her son to continue as long as needed. We often joked that my job was to help her raise Martin.

In diagnostic terms, Martin initially appeared to be suffering from depression, oppositional defiant disorder, and separation anxiety. The diagnostic picture became even more complex as I received information from various medical specialists. For the first few years of treatment, Martin's grief was buried in the middle of these psychiatric disorders.

I initially viewed my approach to treating Martin through both a dynamic and behavioral lens. Martin had experienced an early pattern of trauma in his home that had left him angry and mistrustful. If I could not create a safe emotional harbor for Martin, I knew he would resist coming to counseling or act out in the sessions until I could no longer work with him. This kid also needed significant behavioral interventions. As is true in most therapeutic encounters, my first task was to join the client. My second task was to restructure the thinking and behavioral processes in such a way as to facilitate healthy functioning. Martin needed a great deal of both joining and restructuring.

The length of this case transpired over a period of time when I began to explore brief and solution-focused approaches. I admit that I was initially skeptical of this therapeutic philosophy, since my training had been in more humanistic person-centered therapies. I was also turned off by the evangelical manner of some of my colleagues, who believed any approach other than brief therapy was bordering on the immoral.

I coincidentally had a supervisee during the early months of this case who was a big fan of brief therapy. In order to supervise him adequately I began to read some of the literature. Although I never became a convert to this system of counseling, I did find many of the techniques useful in my work with Martin.

A seven-year case would not seem to qualify me for a place in the Brief Therapy Hall of Fame. If, however, the essence of the brief and solution-focused process is to do no more treatment than is necessary, I believe my work with Martin was in keeping with the spirit of this approach.

Process

<u>Spring, Summer, and Fall, 1989 (Age 9).</u> Establishing rapport with Martin in the early phases of therapy was a walking-on-eggshells dance of knowing when to therapeutically nudge him and when to leave him alone. Some sessions focused on grief; in other sessions, grief was not discussed.

Children as well as adults are given very little time off from their responsibilities after the death of a loved one. Martin was back at school a week after his dad's death. His capacity to concentrate and perform academically was compromised significantly. Martin attended a parochial school known for making kids toe the line. They could be generous with Martin's misbehavior only up to a point.

Martin did not mind that the kids at school knew that his father had died, but he did not want them to know about the suicide. One boy in particular was determined to get Martin to tell him how his father died. Martin relayed to me in an early session that he had made a deal with this nosy fellow. If the kid promised not to ask Martin again how his dad died, Martin agreed to tell him on the last day of school. I asked Martin if he was really comfortable telling this boy the story even if it was the last day of school. Martin looked at me smugly, "I'm not planning on showing up the last day."

School ended for the spring term, and Martin seemed relieved. However, Martin's separation anxiety from his mother began to emerge during these summer months. Emily had enrolled him for two camps during the summer months. Boy Scout camp was scheduled first. Martin became upset at the thought of leaving his mother as the time to depart approached. His reasoning was straightforward: if something happened to his mother, he would have no one left. This is a common fear of bereaved children of all ages.

Martin made a good case for not attending this camp. I supported him on this request but was firm in my belief that he would benefit from the next camp experience, a week-long camp for grieving children. I had referred several children to this camp and all had positive experiences. Martin did attend but did not make it through the entire week. His anxiety over absence from his mother was unbearable. He wrote me a note from camp:

> Dear Pat
>
> I hate it here. I want to come home bad. It is real feelings. I want to come home really bad. I am crying. Please call my mom and tell her. I want to come home on Wednesday.
>
> > Love,
> > Martin

Martin won this battle and came home on Wednesday, returning for the closing ceremony on Saturday. I saw that as "closure" of his camp experience and a positive move.

As school began in the fall, Martin's anxiety about being apart from his mother intensified. His anxiety had become chronic and I had a chance to try a variety of interventions.

One of these interventions allowed Martin to phone his mother at scheduled times so he would know that she was safe. Of course, it was important to have the school's support, and I set up a conference call with Martin's teachers and school administrators. Although they were reluctant to grant special favors, I was able to convince them that Martin needed this consideration during this particularly rough time in his life. I assured them that the calls would not be necessary all year long and that Martin would actually be less disruptive if he was afforded these needed moments of connection with his mother. I probably sounded more certain of success than I actually felt. Although the phoning strategy went on over most of the fall semester, it had the desired effect.

I used solution-focused techniques to help Martin with problems that were manifested in definable behavioral terms. The combination of solution-focused techniques and psychodynamic, supportive, and trust-building approaches became the mainstay of our work together.

Martin discussed his feelings about his dad's death on a regular basis. His grief was intense. He was agitated, irritable, and unfocused and complained of insomnia. His primary physician prescribed a tricyclic antidepressant to help him sleep.

Martin worked on the associative aspect of grief, identifying the many triggers that reminded him of his dad. During a moment of agitation, his mother suggested he write down how he was feeling so he could share it with me. At the next session, he gave me this typed note:

HOW I FEEL IN THE FALL

MY DAD AND I WENT HUNTING LAST FALL. THAT MAKES ME VERY SAD. WHAT ELSE MAKES ME SAD IS THE THINGS WE DID TOGETHER LIKE MAKING THINGS! SCHOOL ALSO REALLY BUGS ME ALOT. IT GETS VERY BORING. I WILL TALK ABOUT THE REST WITH YOU!!

Grieving folks can prepare themselves for the obvious reminders of their loved ones, such as birthdays, holidays, and anniversaries. Unanticipated stimuli can overwhelm with waves of sadness. A smell, a song, or a season of the year can provoke a grief episode in a split second. Fall was a hard season for Martin.

Winter and Spring, 1990 (Age 10). Although Martin's separation anxiety had eased and his ability to talk about his grief had improved, his mood remained unstable. Emily decided he needed an evaluation to rule out bipolar illness, Robert's diagnosis. Although she made a case for getting this assessment, I felt as if I was losing control of Martin's treatment. Martin's highs and lows had a bipolar appearance, but I was unaccustomed to assigning such a complex diagnosis to a child. However, I have learned when working with children to respond supportively to a parent's concerns and act on those concerns whenever possible.

Martin saw a pediatric neurologist who specializes in the treatment of bipolar illness in children. He diagnosed Martin with this disorder and prescribed an antidepressant. If antidepressant medication did not achieve the desired effect, he planned to hospitalize Martin for 30 days and gradually work him into a therapeutic dosage of lithium. Martin reportedly did well in the interview with the specialist until he heard about the possibility of hospitalization. He loudly protested against being in a strange setting away from his mother for that amount of time.

Martin was preoccupied with fear about being hospitalized. I spoke to the neurologist about my concerns regarding Martin's separation anxiety and the negative effect hospitalization might have on Martin's progress. The doctor agreed to use hospitalization only as a last resort, and Martin was relieved. After a few weeks on medication, Martin began to look and act better. He was less impulsive and more able to take responsibility for his behavior. During the first months of the year, he made almost no mention of his father. Although he was more manageable, I began to wonder if the medication was masking his grief. Was he losing the emotional vulnerability that had helped him express his grief? Martin's new level of self-control was tested in April when his mother went into the hospital for surgery. Martin managed this remarkably well.

The symptoms of grief and clinical depression are practically identical. Some grieving people may be coincidentally depressed before their loss. Since Martin's response to the medication was so positive, I had to believe his brain chemistry had needed adjustment.

Martin was stable through the spring, but occasionally the neurologist would make some medication adjustments when Martin's impulsive behavior or sleep disturbances increased. I continued to gently prod him to update me on any new or continuing grief experiences, but Martin did not mention his dad during these months. Martin could have been detached from his grief because of the medication or because of the internalizing of pain that grieving children engage in at this developmental stage. I knew that I had become one of the few people Martin trusted. I would be there when he was ready to share more of his pain.

I used behavioral prescriptions to stop the conflict between Martin and Emily. I suggested that she discriminate as to whether Martin's misbehavior was grief-related, depression-related, or within the normal range of acting out for an adolescent boy. I see this kind of discernment as helping the parent avoid either overreacting or responding insufficiently. Emily became skilled in making these distinctions.

Summer and Fall, 1990 (Age 10). Martin's summer was unremarkable. I spread the time between sessions to every two to three weeks and cut back from 50-minute to 30-minute sessions in order to keep his attention. The pediatric neurologist managing Martin's medication continued to adjust dosages and types of antidepressants, as needed, and was considering hospitalization in order to try him on lithium.

Martin began school with the usual concerns. His new teacher appeared to be somewhat inflexible, and Emily intervened to get her to be more flexible. I supported Emily as I thought appropriate and offered to be available to Martin's teacher.

Although I believed Martin needed special attention, I knew that as he grew older, he would have to adapt to his environment rather than demanding that the environment adapt to him. I wanted Martin to understand how authoritative relationships with teachers, coaches, and other adults could trigger a power struggle. Martin was highly alert to issues of trust. His capacity to trust had been impaired by an erratic relationship with an abusive dad. His challenge was to function with adults whom he did not inherently trust. His tendency was to engage in a power struggle with these adults so he would not have to yield to an authority he believed to be emotionally unsafe. After many months, I helped Martin understand that he made his life more complicated by fighting. He began to understand it was all right not to loudly express every single thought and feeling. He learned to be "politically correct" without necessarily being dishonest. He could afford to lose small battles if he could hang on to his pride.

Martin would demonstrate new maturity and self-control but then unravel emotionally and behaviorally. He was getting in trouble at school and home. Emily became frustrated and called the neurologist, who immediately suggested hospitalization. Although the idea of hospitalization had been discussed, Emily believed that the neurologist was running Martin through a prescribed program and was not really listening to her. She told me that she wanted a new physician, so I referred her to a child psychiatrist at a children's hospital. Martin was scheduled for an assessment in late November.

The psychiatrist changed Martin to a different antidepressant. However, Martin labeled the new doctor as someone he could not trust. He believed the doctor made too many decisions before getting to know him. Martin was put on a waiting list for hospitalization.

Winter and Spring, 1991 (Age 11). Martin vacillated between a new level of emotional maturity and his previous pattern of impulsivity. He looked bipolar to me, with manic and dysphoric phases. His sleep cycles were erratic—sometimes too much sleep, sometimes too little. Martin had been making some improvements in his ability to make friends. He was worried what these new friends would think of him if he went to a hospital for psychiatric problems.

In the session before Martin went to the hospital, he was terribly upset. His spring break would be lost to a hospital stay. He still did not trust the psychiatrist. I advised him to share these feelings directly with the psychiatrist.

I have affiliate privileges at the children's hospital so I was able to see Martin during his one-week stay. Typically, I turn over the primary therapy to the hospital staff and visit the child twice a week to add support, provide continuity, and prepare for return to outpatient counseling.

I do not recall any of my clients who have had a moderate hospital stay. The inpatient experience is either rewarding or miserable. Unfortunately, Martin's experience was in the miserable category. Emily did not believe the medical staff was doing enough. The staff believed Martin's problem was a family issue rather than biochemical. Martin was taken off all medication. He was in group therapy, family therapy, and family group therapy. At discharge he was still not on medication.

The conflict between Emily and the psychiatrist was a familiar one to me. Early in my career, I did a great deal of hospital work. I needed the experience as well as the income. I found hospital work frustrating because of the amount of time I spent triangulated in conflicts between the family and the psychiatrist or the family and the hospital. Martin's case was no different.

After discharge, Martin's behavior got worse. Martin's teacher reported deterioration in his behavior without medication. The psychiatrist started Martin on lithium. Martin did not respond quickly but when an antidepressant was added, Martin gained some control.

Summer and Fall, 1991 (Age 11). Martin and Emily experienced the normal conflicts that come with teen individuation. His growing independence dominated our counseling for months, but he was age appropriate in both still needing his mother and not wanting her involvement.

Two events demonstrated the tension in Martin's process of differentiation. Emily had been having financial problems since her husband's suicide. She was fighting a legal battle to secure Robert's life insurance, which had been denied because his death was a suicide. The case was dragging, and she contemplated selling the house. Martin was angry at her for considering this option. Emily expected Martin to be more understanding of their financial predicament, but his anxiety that his mother might not be able to provide for him was overwhelming.

Martin had a strong reaction when Emily started dating. Martin made it clear that he wanted no men hanging around the house. He was worried she might get hurt. He was also able to discuss his fear of becoming attached to a man who might leave.

Martin entered junior high school in the fall. He was doing better at staying out of trouble. He was adapting to adults rather than hoping they would accommodate. Martin was also building friendships at school and in his neighborhood. He had not been popular in the past due to his acting out. As he gained self-control, he was more attractive.

I was seeing Martin monthly. These visits were checkups, without much content. Occasionally, he presented a specific situation that led to behavioral homework. His trust in the importance of our sessions was solid. Although there was no mention in these months of grief, I was confident that Martin knew he could speak of these matters.

1992 (Age 12). In early winter, Emily and Martin were in a serious automobile wreck. Subsequently, Martin had intense nightmares. He became manic and agitated, although not at the previous level. He took several weeks to get emotionally reorganized. It was hard to know if his reaction was in a normal range or if his early life trauma and loss issues were fueling his response.

Generally, Martin was improving. His cycles of agitation and depression were less intense. His acting out at school was designed to get attention as opposed to the severe decompensating episodes of earlier years. During 1992, Emily often attended sessions with him. Martin was no longer suffering from separation anxiety. He just didn't need her as much any more, but Emily wasn't ready to be fired from parenting duties. His behavior toward her was developing to the diagnosable level of Oppositional Defiant Disorder.

In keeping with a solution-focused approach, I encouraged Martin and Emily to explore exceptions to old patterns of conflict and isolated the variables that created successful interactions. Contracts for minimal behavioral expectations were written and posted on the refrigerator. Meanwhile Emily had begun training to be a therapist and spoke to Martin in a therapeutic and analytic style that irritated Martin extremely. Emily took the hint and reverted to the basic rule of communication with a teen: deliver the message clearly and in 90 seconds or less.

1993 (Age 13). I saw Martin 16 times in 1993. These sessions continued the independence theme. Martin was managing most areas of his life fairly well. The young entrepreneur proudly brought his "Lawn Care by Martin" brochure to a session.

In the spring, around the time of the fourth anniversary of his dad's death, Martin began to talk about his grief. He had not done so in many months. He mused about who he would be now if his dad had not died. He wondered which of his personality traits he had inherited from his dad, for good or worse.

I was touched by Martin's questions. I encouraged him to imagine what his life might have been like if his father had lived. We explored both the positive and negative possibilities. This conversation helped Martin construct realistic instead of fantasized memories. He remembered both his strong attachment to his father and his fear of his father. I was again reminded of the importance of seeing grieving children into their adolescent years. Martin now had the maturity to handle painful emotions.

1994, 1995, and 1996 (Age 14–16). Martin came for nine sessions in 1994, five in 1995, and five more in 1996. Emily was not out of line in her belief about the amount of parenting a 16-year-old should need, but Martin was functioning so well that she did not have much concrete evidence to support her case. Besides, she was busy working and going to school. Individuation was happening.

Usually the therapy sessions were a time of ventilation and subsequent realignment of their relationship. The conflict would die down temporarily. Although these episodes were tough on Emily, she was truly grateful that Martin had caught up developmentally and was healthy enough to struggle with her in an age-appropriate way.

Martin was still on medication, but a new psychiatrist Martin liked and trusted had taken over. He was compliant with taking medication.

Martin was now in high school. He attended an academically challenging parochial school. He studied hard and made good grades. He became involved in the foreign exchange program and hosted a student from Germany. Consequently, he made a summer trip to Germany to visit his friend. His ability to handle this type of complex activity without much help from an adult was remarkable.

In 1995 and 1996, I scheduled Martin on a "call as needed" basis. Martin usually came by himself but was willing to include his mother if she expressed the need. Martin used his sessions to focus on a specific issue. He presented a problem and allowed me to help him explore options. He left with a plan.

1997 (Age 17). Recently, Martin has been talking about the isolation he feels from peers. He continues in Alateen and is committed to abstinence from drugs and alcohol. The isolation results from the fact that many high schoolers do not share this commitment. Martin is determined to invest in friendships that will not lead in the direction of substance use, and he is getting results. I think that a 17-year-old experiencing isolation over unwillingness to succumb to peer pressure to drink is an acceptable problem to have to solve.

Outcome

Martin's case is not closed. I suspect I will continue to see him from time to time in the format that has become familiar to us. Martin calls or asks Emily to set up an appointment. He presents a problem and we collaboratively generate solutions. I expect that Emily will see me on occasion regarding her concerns about their relationship.

As this case study is being written, I consider Martin's counseling to have accomplished the original goals for therapy as well as those goals that evolved over time. Martin is, for the most part, emotionally stable and self-disciplined. He forms meaningful attachments with carefully selected adults and peers. He balances work and play. On his own initiative, he attends Alateen.

Martin struggles in many areas. He still experiences mood swings and he must use all of his cognitive and behavioral tools to keep his anger in check. The grief over his dad's death sneaks into his awareness from time to time. I believe he will need to revisit his grief experience more intensely in his adult years.

Discussion

Martin required a counseling relationship based on trust. Without Martin's confidence that he was in a secure therapeutic environment, he would not have taken steps away from habitual patterns. He would have "won" the power struggles created by his perception that I, like other adults, wanted to control him. Although I was often unsure of what to do with Martin, I knew not to rush or push.

This trusting relationship provided a platform from which to use other tools. Behavioral prescriptions, solution-focused techniques, and psychoeducational approaches were interspersed with classic person-centered reflective listening to create a balance between rapport and therapeutic movement.

I have wondered what "role," if any, I played. I wanted to avoid the father-figure role because it was fraught with emotional complications due to Martin's painful experiences with his dad. Instead, the role of an interested and kindly uncle felt right to me. As an "uncle," I could be part of the family without too much intimacy or too many expectations. I was always conscious of being a role model for Martin since there were few males involved with him. I specifically tried to model respect whenever I communicated with his mother.

The initial months of treatment were anything but smooth. There were chaotic periods that undermined my confidence. There were other health-care providers involved in this case whom neither I nor my clients completely trusted. There were uncontrollable external events such as the car accident. The level of productive counseling at which we finally arrived was achieved through an unwillingness to give up.

I saw Martin in a restaurant a few months ago. I was with my family and we were seated at the table next to his. He was with a friend and the friend's father. We stood to shake hands. Here was a strong, good-looking young man who almost matched my tall frame. He did not introduce me to his table, and my family knows not to ask when I do not introduce them to people we meet in public. There was an unspoken warmth between us. I felt proud. Martin had been raised under difficult circumstances and had turned out well.

Biographical Statement

Patrick O'Malley, PhD, is licensed as a professional counselor and a marriage family therapist. He has been in practice in Fort Worth, Texas, since 1979. He is a clinical member and an approved supervisor with the American Association for Marriage and Family Therapy (AAMFT) and has served as chair of AAMFT's Ethics Committee and as a member of AAMFT's Ethics Code Revision Task Force. Pat has developed a training model for volunteer facilitators at a nonprofit center for grieving children and their families in Fort Worth called The WARM Place. You can reach Pat at nomalley1@aol.com.

Index